MISSION
MEETS
MARKET

A Sales and Marketing Playbook for Education Nonprofits

GRAMMAR
FACTORY
— EST? 2013 —

MISSION MEETS MARKET

JAY BAKHRU

Published by Grammar Factory Publishing, an imprint of MacMillan
Company Limited.

Grammar Factory Publishing
MacMillan Company Limited
25 Telegram Mews, 39th Floor, Suite 3906
Toronto, Ontario, Canada
M5V 3Z1

www.grammarfactory.com

Bakhru, Jay.
Mission Meets Market: A Sales and Marketing Playbook for
Education Nonprofits / Jay Bakhru.

Paperback ISBN 978-1-998528-42-4
Hardcover ISBN 978-1-998528-44-8
eBook ISBN 978-1-998528-43-1

1. BUS074000. Business & Economics / Nonprofit Organizations &
Charities / General.
2. EDU034000. Education / Administration / General.
3. BUS058000. Business & Economics / Sales & Selling / General.

Production Credits
Cover design by Designerbility
Interior layout design by Setareh Ashrafologhalai
Book production and editorial services by Grammar Factory Publishing

Grammar Factory's Carbon Neutral Publishing Commitment
Grammar Factory Publishing is proud to be neutralizing the carbon
footprint of all printed copies of its authors' books printed by or ordered
directly through Grammar Factory or its affiliated companies through the
purchase of Gold Standard-Certified International Offsets.

Disclaimer
The material in this publication is of the nature of general comment only
and does not represent professional advice. It is not intended to provide
specific guidance for particular circumstances, and it should not be relied
on as the basis for any decision to take action or not take action on any
matter which it covers. Readers should obtain professional advice where
appropriate, before making any such decision. To the maximum extent
permitted by law, the author and publisher disclaim all responsibility and
liability to any person, arising directly or indirectly from any person taking
or not taking action based on the information in this publication.

DISCLAIMER

SOME NAMES of people and organizations and specific details described have been changed to protect confidentiality.

To the nonprofit education leaders whose courage and creativity shape brighter futures, and to the students who inspire us every day—this book is for you.

CONTENTS

FOREWORD

WE DIDN'T SET out to become sales and marketing experts.

Like many in the education and nonprofit world, our backgrounds are in teaching, policy, entrepreneurship, and system change—not pitch decks or product positioning. And yet, time and again, we've found ourselves in conversations with leaders trying to make their work more sustainable, scalable, and influential.

The challenge? The path to that kind of impact often runs straight through the world of sales and marketing.

That's what makes this book so timely—and so necessary. *Mission Meets Market* offers something we haven't seen before: a clear, honest, and practical guide to revenue generation for mission-driven organizations working in complex education systems. It's not about "selling out." It's about showing up—with clarity, intention, and strategy—in the markets your work depends on.

We've each approached this challenge from different angles. Jeff came to this work through a mix of policy, philanthropy, and innovation leadership—first as an entrepreneur, then as a senior executive at McGraw-Hill Education, and now as a partner at EdSolutions. He's seen how hard it is to bring good ideas to scale without a strategy for engaging markets—and how transformative it can be when organizations get that part right.

Beth's journey started in the classroom, then wound through publishing houses, product teams, and customer experience roles. Over two decades, she's led the development and launch of educational tools used by millions of students. Through it all, she's seen how essential it is to align strong pedagogy with a clear value proposition that meets the real needs of schools and systems.

Together, we co-founded EdSolutions alongside Jay Bakhru with a shared belief: that market dynamics, when approached with integrity, can be a force for equity. And that nonprofit leaders deserve better tools, language, and support for navigating those dynamics.

We also knew we couldn't do it alone. Over the years, we've been fortunate to build an extraordinary team—former educators, nonprofit and for-profit executives, strategists, and researchers—who bring deep experience and a shared commitment to helping mission-driven organizations grow, sustain, and scale their impact. This book draws on the wisdom, tools, and lessons that have emerged from that collective work. It reflects what we've learned—together with our team and our clients—about what it takes to build something that lasts.

That's what this book offers. Jay, who authored *Mission Meets Market*, has spent years in the trenches—first as a nonprofit founder, then as a trusted advisor to organizations across the education landscape. His writing distills the patterns we've seen again and again: brilliant ideas getting stuck because they lack a sales plan; passionate teams burning out because their funding isn't built to last.

This book is here to help. It's here to challenge old assumptions, offer new tools, and remind you that mission and market don't have to be at odds.

Whether you're just starting to explore earned revenue or looking to grow a thriving, mission-aligned sales operation, we hope this book meets you where you are. More than that, we hope it makes you feel less alone. Because building something that lasts—something that changes lives and shifts systems—is hard. But it's also possible.

We're proud to share *Mission Meets Market* with you. And we're excited to see where it takes you next.

JEFF LIVINGSTON & BETH MEJIA

Partners, EdSolutions

INTRODUCTION
Why Sales and Marketing Matter for Mission-Driven Organizations

IT WAS NEARLY seven in the evening, at the end of a very long day. Alicia, the executive director of CivicRoots, stared at the glow of her laptop, the office around her long emptied of her passionate but exhausted team. Her fingertips tapped anxiously against the cold metal of her desk.

She knew that the organization's civics curriculum was extraordinary: teachers raved about how it sparked lively debates, inspired critical thinking, and transformed passive students into active, informed citizens. Yet the numbers on the screen were unyielding. Customer growth had stalled again this quarter, and financial reserves had dwindled to a trickle.

She exhaled deeply, pushing back her hair and glancing at the framed photographs lining her shelves: smiling groups of students holding handmade signs about democracy, civic pride shining from their eyes. Alicia's heart panged with frustration and sadness. "We built something that truly matters," she murmured softly. "So why can't we reach more schools?"

Her phone buzzed, and Alicia's pulse quickened when she saw the caller ID: it was Emma, her philanthropic program officer from the FuturePromise Foundation. Emma had always been supportive, but Alicia knew that these recent results could test even the strongest partnerships.

Alicia picked up the phone. "Hi Emma," she said, trying to muster a note of optimism in her weary voice.

"Evening, Alicia." Emma's tone was gentle, but carried a subtle tension. "I reviewed your latest report. I know how hard you're working, and your impact stories are powerful, but we need to see growth in reach soon."

Alicia's chest tightened. "I know, Emma. And we're trying everything—teachers love it, but scaling has been a challenge."

"I completely understand the struggle," Emma responded sympathetically. "Look, we truly believe in your mission, but our trustees need assurance that CivicRoots is sustainable. Let's strategize ways to enhance your outreach. I'll help however I can."

After the call ended, Alicia sat still, Emma's supportive yet firm words resonating. She felt caught between her passion for educating civic-minded citizens, and the relentless financial realities of nonprofit leadership. She leaned back and closed her eyes, memories flooding in—like the morning she watched a formerly quiet ninth grader eloquently debate civic responsibilities before the city council, or the handwritten note from a teacher saying, "Your curriculum changed my students' lives." Alicia clung to those moments as motivation.

Yet, despite these powerful memories, her anxiety persisted, twisting tightly in her chest. She knew the challenges ahead were daunting, and in that moment she felt deeply discouraged, overwhelmed, and uncertain. Staring at the photographs once more, Alicia whispered, almost to herself, "What am I supposed to do next?"

IF YOU'RE READING THIS, chances are that you relate deeply to Alicia's struggle.

You lead an education-focused nonprofit doing incredible work. You wake up each morning driven by a powerful mission: improving outcomes for students, supporting teachers, and transforming schools and districts.

But there's a problem—and it's one that probably keeps you up at night more often than you'd like to admit. Despite the importance and value of what your organization offers, you are struggling to generate enough sales and revenue.

Perhaps you've sat in board meetings facing uncomfortable questions from philanthropic funders about revenue generation, or seen confusion on potential customers' faces as you attempt to describe the value of your program. You might have even tried adopting some standard-issue marketing tactics—redesigning your website, running ads, hiring salespeople, and so on—but still found yourself financially stuck and, even worse, feeling like you're selling out the values that made you pursue this mission in the first place.

You're not alone. This is one of the most common challenges faced by nonprofit leaders.

The National Center on Charitable Statistics reveals that approximately 30% of nonprofits cease to exist after ten years.[1] And, according to *Forbes*, over half of all nonprofits that are chartered are destined to fail or stall within a few years due to leadership issues and lack of a strategic plan.[2]

1   Greg McRay, "Top 5 Reasons Why Nonprofits Fail," 501c3.org, accessed September 3, 2025, https://www.501c3.org/top-5-reasons-why-nonprofits-fail/.

2   Ian Altman, "Half of Nonprofits are Setup to Fail: How About Your Favorite?," *Forbes*, March 20, 2016, https://www.forbes.com/sites/ianaltman/2016/03/20/half-of-nonprofits-are-setup-to-fail-how-about-your-favorite/.

Even among those nonprofits that do manage to achieve sustainability, most fail to scale their impact effectively. According to a study published in the *Stanford Social Innovation Review*, only 11% of organizations have fully earned the right to scale by mastering all components of strategic leadership.[3]

This isn't just a business concern—it's a moral imperative. In education, failing to scale means that countless students miss out on transformative learning experiences that could positively impact their futures. We have a duty to ensure that the best, most effective learning solutions reach the kids who need them most.

And here's the reality: in today's rapidly evolving educational landscape, relying solely on grants and donations is akin to building a house on shifting sands. Public funding is unpredictable, philanthropic priorities change, and competition for limited resources is fiercer than ever. To navigate these uncertainties and secure your organization's future, focusing on *earned revenue*—that is, income generated from selling goods or services related to your mission—isn't just advisable. It's essential.

Earned revenue provides a stable financial foundation that empowers your nonprofit to plan ahead, invest in growth, and amplify your impact. By developing sustainable revenue streams, you reduce dependency on external funding and gain greater control over your organization's destiny.

Part of the problem is that for most (if not all) of those people who have dedicated themselves to transforming K–12 education and beyond, sales and marketing can feel uncomfortable, unnatural, and even morally at odds with why they joined the nonprofit sector in the first place.

---

3   "Study: Most Nonprofits Lacking in Leadership, Management," *The NonProfit Times*, November 1, 2017, https://thenonprofittimes.com/npt_articles/study-nonprofits-lacking-leadership-management/.

That's hardly surprising. The plain fact is that most sales and marketing playbooks were written for profit-maximizing companies, not mission-driven organizations. They assume that all customers will behave like consumers; that growth is always the goal, no matter the cost; and that the loudest and strongest voice always wins. Those are definitely *not* the kinds of values that can help build community and shape the next generation of civic-minded citizens.

That's the reason why I wrote this book: to help nonprofit leaders like you get better at selling and marketing your organization in ways that are authentic, mission-aligned, and ultimately transformative for the communities you serve. This isn't about becoming a different kind of leader—it's about expanding your toolkit so you can lead more powerfully and sustainably.

Let me be clear: generating earned revenue as a nonprofit leader is absolutely possible. I've seen it happen again and again. I've worked with nonprofits that started out with a few pilot partners, and now have multi-year contracts with dozens of districts. I've watched organizations that once relied almost entirely on philanthropy now fund half their budget through services that schools and systems are eager to pay for. I've seen leaders just like you—mission-driven, equity-centered, and perhaps skeptical of the whole notion of earned revenue at first—build sales strategies that not only brought in new revenue, but also deepened their impact.

Picture this: you walk into a funder meeting and, instead of worrying about your year-end gap, you discuss how to extend a fee-for-service model that's already generating steady income. Or maybe a district leader reaches out to you not because you chased them down, but because they've heard from peers about the tangible outcomes you're delivering. You hire confidently, knowing that revenue isn't an open question. You say no to projects that don't fit. You lead with clarity.

This book won't give you a silver bullet to solve every single challenge you will face. But it will give you the tools to build a strategy that works—for your mission, your team, and the communities you serve.

So, at this point, you're almost certainly wondering—who am I, and how can I help you achieve this?

I'm a co-founder and one of three partners at EdSolutions, an education-focused social-impact consulting firm I launched alongside my colleagues Jeff Livingston and Beth Mejia. Together, we lead a team that works with non-profits, philanthropies, and government agencies to design and scale innovative solutions in public education. Over the years, I've had the privilege of supporting hundreds of mission-driven organizations across the K–12 landscape, helping them grow their impact while building stronger and more sustainable financial foundations.

However, I didn't start in consulting: I began my career as a teacher, made my way into the business world by leading marketing for a major educational publisher, and later founded and ran a nonprofit initiative called the Center for Education Market Dynamics. Along the way, I've launched ventures that have taken off, as well as a few that didn't. At all.

Through each success and stumble, I've come to believe that nonprofit leaders like you and me are *builders*. We test, revise, adapt, and try again. We learn to lead with both our heads and our hearts. So, what I'm offering you with this book is shaped by real-world lessons and a deep respect for the wisdom you already carry.

EdSolutions itself is built from that same mix of lived experience, entrepreneurial trial and error, and deep sector expertise. Our team includes former teachers and school leaders, marketing professionals and nonprofit operators, philanthropic strategists and systems thinkers. We've sat

Figure Intro.1: MissionMarket Model – The 10 Steps to Build Your Sustainability Plan

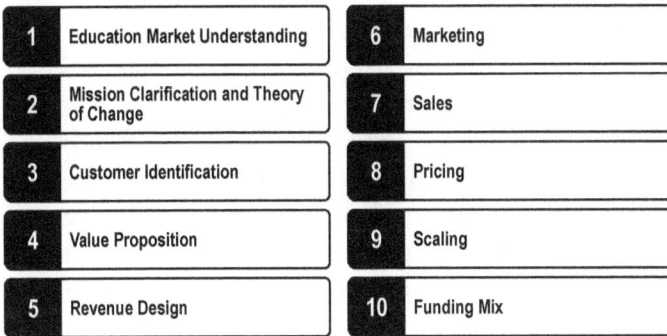

1	Education Market Understanding	**6**	Marketing
2	Mission Clarification and Theory of Change	**7**	Sales
3	Customer Identification	**8**	Pricing
4	Value Proposition	**9**	Scaling
5	Revenue Design	**10**	Funding Mix

in your seat, pitched great solutions, and still been told no. We've wrestled with how to price with equity, how to stay true to mission in a sales conversation, and how to create clarity in a crowded market.

That's why we created the **MissionMarket Model**—a framework built specifically for education nonprofit leaders like you, designed to help you grow your earned revenue without compromising your purpose.

What is the MissionMarket Model?

The MissionMarket Model is a ten-part roadmap that is designed to help you create your organization's **Sustainability Plan**—that is, to transform your scattered sales efforts into a strategic, mission-aligned revenue engine. It gives you the tools, language, and structure to bring your work to the people who need it most—districts, schools, funders, and intermediaries—while sustaining your organization financially.

Whether you're selling professional learning, tech tools, research, or direct services, the MissionMarket Model will help you:

- clarify your niche,
- communicate your value,
- reach the right customers,
- convert interest into sustainable revenue, and
- grow with systems, not stress.

The MissionMarket Model isn't theory: it's been tested and refined through years of real-world work with education nonprofits navigating today's complex landscape. It recognizes that your mission is your North Star—and that earned revenue, when done right, is a powerful vehicle for expanding your impact. This model is here to help you build the future you believe in, with strategy, confidence, and financial resilience.

The chapters ahead will walk you through each step of the MissionMarket Model. Here's a quick overview of each component:

1. Understand the K–12 education sector

Before you can successfully sell into the education space, you need to understand how that space works. The first step of the MissionMarket Model is dedicated to demystifying the sector's unique landscape—how funding flows, who holds decision-making power, how procurement processes work, and where philanthropy fits into the equation. Once you have a clear picture of the system, you can navigate it with greater confidence and purpose.

2. Start with your mission and theory of change

Revenue should serve your mission, not steer it. This step helps you clarify your theory of change and use it as the foundation for your earned revenue strategy. By connecting your offerings to the outcomes you seek, you ensure that every dollar earned is aligned with your broader goals.

3. Identify your target customers

Not every school, district, or funder is the right fit. In this step, you'll learn how to segment the market, build customer personas, and focus your efforts on the audiences most likely to benefit from your work—and those that are most ready to say yes.

4. Define your value proposition and positioning

In a crowded field of well-meaning providers, clarity is your competitive edge. This component of the MissionMarket Model helps you craft a value proposition that speaks directly to your customers' needs and position your work in ways that feel relevant, compelling, and distinct.

5. Design a revenue model that fits

One size does *not* fit all. This chapter explores nonprofit-compatible revenue models—such as service-based pricing, subscriptions, government contracts, and hybrid approaches—and guides you toward a model that works for your mission, your customers, and your operational capacity.

6. Market with intention (and integrity)

Marketing doesn't have to feel slick or sales-y. This step focuses on building trust and awareness through channels that work for nonprofits—email, events, peer networks, and thoughtful content. You'll learn how to reach the right people, with the right message, at the right time.

7. Sell with purpose, not pressure

Sales can be values-driven and human-centered. In this step, we break down how to run effective discovery conversations, qualify leads, handle objections, and close deals—all while staying grounded in your mission. You'll learn how to guide potential partners through a decision-making journey that feels clear and collaborative.

8. Price for equity and sustainability

Pricing is both an emotional and a strategic decision. In this step, we help you move away from underpricing out of guilt or fear and develop pricing strategies rooted in value, fairness, and long-term sustainability. You'll learn how to integrate equity into your pricing decisions while ensuring financial health for your organization.

9. Scale what works, sustainably

Growth shouldn't come at the expense of quality or team well-being. This chapter focuses on operationalizing your earned revenue efforts—mapping workflows, assigning roles, choosing tools, and creating systems that let you deliver consistently as demand increases.

10. Explore mixed funding models

In the final step, we zoom out to consider how earned revenue fits within a broader funding strategy. You'll explore how to blend revenue from philanthropy, government contracts, partnerships, and fee-for-service in ways that create a more resilient and balanced financial model.

Plan of the book

In addition to learning each step of the MissionMarket Model in detail, each chapter will introduce you to scenarios featuring nonprofit leaders—composites drawn from dozens of real-world organizations—who are facing the same challenges you are. These short narratives will hopefully serve not only to help bring the concepts we'll be discussing to life, but also to remind you that you're not alone. Every pain point you've felt—confusion about pricing, anxiety around pitching, frustration with inconsistent sales—is one that other mission-driven leaders have faced, too. And just like you, they are learning how to navigate those challenges with courage and clarity.

Throughout the book, you'll find several features designed to help you apply these ideas to your own organization. Each chapter ends with "Reflection Questions"—simple but thought-provoking prompts to help you connect the material to your day-to-day leadership. These questions are more than just conversation starters: together, they provide a structured pathway to building your organization's Sustainability Plan.

To support that journey, we've also created a complimentary workbook to help you create that Sustainability Plan—available for download on the EdSolutions website at https://edsolutions.com/mission-meets-market—that includes tools aligned to each chapter. From customer segmentation templates to revenue model checklists, these tools will help you move from insight to action. If you work through the full set of Reflection Questions and use the workbook alongside this book, you'll end up with a comprehensive, mission-aligned Sustainability Plan tailored to your organization's strengths and goals.

Also included throughout the chapters are "Action Steps" to help you put ideas into motion. These are short, practical exercises you can do as you read the book (or shortly after you finish it) to deepen your thinking and apply key concepts to your own organization.

Finally, to help you see how it all comes together, you'll also find an example of a completed Sustainability Plan in the appendix, based on the story of Alicia and the fictional nonprofit CivicRoots we met above. Think of this sample plan as a concrete example of how the pieces can fit together in real life: hopefully, it can be a helpful reference for you as you build your own Sustainability Plan.

Taken together, these tools, prompts, and insights are here to help you not just learn the MissionMarket Model, but *use* it.

A quick note before we begin: if you're already a) well-versed in the structure of the K–12 education sector, and/or b) your organization already has a clear theory of change in place, feel free to skip past Chapters 1 and 2. Those components provide the strong and essential foundation that the MissionMarket Model then builds upon, but if this is ground that you've already sufficiently covered in your own organization, you can move directly to those sections that feel most urgent for your work. (However, if you're up for a refresher on the lay of the education landscape, or want to run your existing theory of change through the step-by-step formulation we detail in Chapter 2, by all means do so!)

And finally, a point of clarification. Most of the examples in this book derive from the K–12 education space, because that's where my own personal experience runs deepest. But, if you lead a nonprofit working outside of K–12, you'll find that the core challenges—and the strategies to address them—are strikingly similar to those we cover in the pages ahead. Sales and marketing may look a bit different in each setting, but the foundational ideas in this book—clarifying your value, identifying your customer, and designing a mission-aligned revenue model—apply across all levels of education. Our team at EdSolutions brings expertise that spans the full education continuum, from early childhood through postsecondary and workforce development.

Wherever you sit in the education ecosystem, you're here because you're building something that matters. Maybe it's a program to support new educators, a tool to improve student outcomes, or an initiative to connect learners to good jobs. Whatever it is, somewhere out there is a district that needs your solution. A student who will thrive because of your work. A funder looking for the kind of clarity and conviction only you can provide.

Whether you're just getting started, or looking to fine-tune an already successful program, the chapters ahead are designed to meet you where you are, and help you move forward with confidence. This book will give you a clear roadmap, tested tools, and the encouragement to keep going when the road gets bumpy. It will help you connect your purpose to the people, partners, and systems that can help it scale.

You don't have to choose between mission and market. You can lead with both.

So, let's get down to it. Because the work you have ahead of you is too important to wait.

1

UNDERSTANDING THE EDUCATION SECTOR
How K–12 Markets (and Beyond) Really Work

WHEN MARCUS AND PRIYA launched SparkScience, they were certain they had a game-changer.

Marcus, a former middle school science teacher, had spent years watching students disengage from dry, textbook-based instruction. He dreamed of something better—something hands-on and inquiry-driven. Priya, a brilliant software engineer who'd built interactive platforms for biotech firms, had the skills to bring that dream to life. Together, they had created a project-based science learning platform where students could design experiments, track real-time data, and collaborate across classrooms.

Their pilot school raved about it. One teacher called it "the first time my students actually *begged* for more science."

So, why weren't more schools signing on?

Marcus had assumed that his years in the classroom would give SparkScience a leg up but, as it turned out, knowing the inside of a school didn't mean understanding how districts *buy*. He didn't know which titles held budget authority, or that many purchasing decisions were made months in advance, long before he and Priya could ever get in the room. He kept reaching out to principals in their target districts directly, all the while not realizing that purchasing authority sat with the assistant superintendent's office.

Priya, meanwhile, was baffled by the whole ecosystem. She was used to linear B2B sales cycles and clear product-market fit. "Why would a district need a three-month pilot *and* board approval just to buy a $15-per-student license?" she once asked during a team meeting. She kept trying to build an ever-slicker product, hoping better features would win the day.

But features weren't the issue. The central problem was that neither she nor Marcus really understood the system they were trying to sell into. They had the right solution, but they didn't know who the decision-makers were, how budgets flowed, or what barriers stood in their way. No matter how strong the pedagogy or polished the tech, without that crucial knowledge, their whole enterprise would remain stalled.

MARCUS AND PRIYA'S STORY is far from unique. If you're leading a nonprofit in the education space, chances are you've felt the frustration of seeing a great idea go nowhere simply because you couldn't find the right door, the right person, or the right moment. Maybe your program was successfully piloted in one school, and then simply vanished into the ether the following year. Or maybe you spent months pitching a funder, only to realize you were offering a solution they couldn't fund—or, worse, didn't understand.

Before you can sell anything—whether it's a curriculum product, a teacher professional development (PD) program, or a whole new model for student support—you have to understand the system you're trying to change. That's why the first step of the MissionMarket Model is to provide you with a field guide of the complex, multi-tiered world of U.S. K-12 education—who the players are, where the money comes from, how decisions are made, and how philanthropic priorities shape what's possible.

NOTE TO READERS

Although this chapter focuses on the K–12 sector, many of the principles—market fragmentation, funding complexity, decentralized decision-making—hold true across the broader education continuum, including early childhood, higher education, and workforce training. If your work spans these domains, keep reading: the chapters ahead will help you apply the MissionMarket Model across sectors.

And, as I mentioned in the Introduction, if you're already well-versed in the organizational landscape of K–12 education, you may want to move on to Chapter 2 or 3.

The U.S. K–12 education landscape: A patchwork of models

The term "K-12 education" can give the illusion that what you're dealing with is a single, coherent system. But in reality it's a tangled web of different school types, governance structures, and local variations.

For our current purposes, we will cover only the major nodes in that network, along with the pros and cons that each offers as a market for your education product or service. Keep in mind, however, that each of these branches outward to create their own, sometimes bewilderingly complex sub-networks.

Public schools
Public schools are the backbone of the K-12 system, serving over 80% of U.S. students.[4] Funded by a mix of federal, state, and local dollars, they are governed by elected school boards and run by district administrations. But don't be fooled by that "public" label—every district is its own little kingdom, with unique needs, priorities, and procurement rules.

Charter schools
Charter schools are publicly funded, but independently operated. Some are single-site schools, while others belong to large charter management organizations (CMOs). They often have more flexibility around curriculum, staffing, and operations, which can make them faster adopters of new products or approaches. However, they can also be fragmented and hard to scale across.

Private schools
Private schools educate about 10% of U.S. students, and are funded largely through tuition and philanthropy. While they offer greater autonomy and faster buying cycles, they're a smaller slice of the market, and typically operate outside of state-mandated curriculum and assessments.

Alternative and nontraditional models
This category includes virtual schools, micro-schools, home-schooling networks, and hybrid models, many of which expanded after the Covid-19 pandemic. These are often early adopters of innovative products, but they also lack centralized purchasing structures.

---

4   "U.S. Public, Private and Charter Schools in 5 Charts," Pew Research Center, June 6, 2024, https://www.pewresearch.org/short-reads/2024/06/06/us-public-private-and-charter-schools-in-5-charts/.

Families (B2C)

An often overlooked but growing part of the education market is direct-to-consumer (B2C) sales to families. Parents are increasingly purchasing supplemental learning tools, tutoring, and enrichment programs outside of the school system, ranging from reading and math apps to test prep and learning pods. While individual sales are smaller and customer acquisition can be expensive, this model offers more flexibility and less red tape than institutional sales, and can be an important diversification strategy for nonprofits with strong parent-facing offerings.

After-school and out-of-school programs

Community-based organizations, youth nonprofits, and expanded learning providers serve millions of students outside the traditional school day. These programs often operate in partnership with schools or receive funding through public grants (e.g., 21st Century Community Learning Centers), city budgets, or philanthropy. They are a major consumer of supplemental curriculum, social-emotional learning (SEL) programs, and enrichment-focused professional development. These organizations are often more open to innovation, and the buying processes can be quicker. However, they also typically work with tighter budgets.

What do schools buy?

Now that we've provisionally mapped the landscape of the education market, we can define what exactly it is that you're attempting to sell into that market.

If you're selling to schools, your offering likely falls into one or more of the following four categories:

1. Curriculum

- **Core curriculum**—these are the primary instructional materials in subjects like math, English language arts, science, and social studies. Core adoptions are high-stakes, multi-year decisions, often made through formal RFP processes every five to seven years. They typically require alignment to state standards, rigorous evidence of efficacy, and approval by school boards or curriculum committees. Examples include *Eureka Math* (Great Minds), *StudySync* (McGraw Hill), or *Amplify Science.*

- **Supplemental curriculum**—these tools are used to reinforce, extend, or differentiate core instruction; think programs like *Newsela* for reading, *Prodigy Math* for math, or *BrainPOP* for interactive content. They're easier to pilot and purchase, often coming out of school- or department-level budgets rather than district-wide adoption cycles. But while the sales process can be quicker, the market is more fragmented and budgets are tighter.

2. Assessment

- **Formative assessments**—these are low-stakes tools that help educators understand how students are progressing and allow them to adjust instruction accordingly. They're often built into instructional programs or provided as standalone platforms. Examples include Kahoot!, Formative by Newsela, Nearpod, Amplify (mCLASS), McGraw Hill (Achieve3000 Literacy), and Carnegie Learning (MATHia).

- **Summative assessments**—these measure student learning at the end of an instructional period (often for accountability purposes), and are usually mandated by state education departments. Examples include state tests aligned to ESSA requirements (like the *Smarter Balanced Assessment Consortium* or *Texas STAAR*), as well as national assessments like *NAEP* or *ACCESS for ELLs* for English learners. These assessments can shape district purchasing priorities in significant ways.

3. Professional development

From one-off workshops to year-long coaching programs, professional development is a multibillion-dollar market, and nearly every district allocates funds toward it. These offerings target educators across the spectrum: classroom teachers, instructional coaches, school leaders, and sometimes district administrators. They span all grade levels, from early childhood to high school, and can focus on content-specific instruction (like math or reading), pedagogical strategies, culturally responsive teaching, or social-emotional learning.

4. Edtech

Education technology (edtech) is the digital layer that supports everything from curriculum delivery and assessment to data tracking, student engagement, and school—home communication. The category is broad, and growing. It includes learning management systems like Google Classroom and Canvas, assessment platforms like Khan Academy or i-Ready, data dashboards like Schoolzilla, and communication tools like Remind or ClassDojo. It also includes more specialized tools: adaptive math platforms like Zearn, AI-powered writing support like Quill, or SEL tools like Along.

Who in the education sector pays for these products?

The short answer is "it depends." The longer answer involves some combination of the below:

Federal funding

Federal funding makes up less than 10% of overall K–12 spending, but it plays a crucial role—especially because it is highly targeted and often tied to specific student populations. These dollars are typically allocated through formulas or competitive grants and come with strict guidelines about how they can be used. Key streams include:

- **Title I**: Designed to support schools serving high percentages of students from low-income families, Title I funds are aimed at closing achievement gaps. They can be used for interventions, instructional supports, family engagement, and other efforts that improve student outcomes in high-need schools.

- **Title II**: Focused on improving teacher and principal quality, Title II funding supports professional development and recruitment efforts. Districts can use these funds to provide evidence-based training, coaching, and leadership development aimed at increasing the effectiveness of educators and ultimately improving student achievement.

- **Title III**: Designed to support English learners and immigrant students, Title III funding helps schools provide language instruction, academic support, and family engagement initiatives. The goal is to help English learners attain English proficiency and meet the same challenging academic standards as their peers.

- **Title IV**: Aimed at supporting a well-rounded education, Title IV funds can be used across a wide range of priorities, from STEM education to school safety, technology, and mental health services. The program helps schools build student-centered learning environments that promote academic success and healthy development.

- **IDEA (Individuals with Disabilities Education Act)**: IDEA funds provide resources for students with disabilities, ensuring they receive the services and accommodations guaranteed under federal law. These dollars often fund special education staff, assistive technology, and individualized instructional support.

For nonprofits, aligning your offerings to one or more of these funding streams—especially Title I or IDEA—can make it easier for districts to find a viable funding source to pay for your work. But be aware: each stream comes with compliance requirements and reporting expectations that can affect how your services are structured and delivered.

State funding

State funding typically makes up the largest share of a public school's budget. Each state has its own formula to determine how dollars are distributed, often factoring in enrollment, local tax capacity, and the needs of specific student groups (such as English learners, students with disabilities, or rural communities).

But states do more than allocate money—they set the rules of the game. State education agencies decide academic standards, drive major policy shifts, and establish the frameworks that shape district priorities. That's why understanding your target state's education priorities is essential for crafting a strategy that resonates.

When your offerings align with these priorities—whether through curriculum, professional development, or research support—you're much more likely to gain traction. And when they don't? Even the best-designed solution can fall flat.

Local funding

Local property taxes often fund a significant portion of public school budgets—which, unsurprisingly, leads to stark disparities between districts. Affluent communities may have modern facilities, low student-to-teacher ratios, and ample budgets for enrichment programs. Meanwhile, just a few miles away, a lower-income district might be operating with aging textbooks, limited support staff, and no discretionary funds for innovation.

These disparities shape not only what districts can afford, but also how they prioritize spending. A suburban district with stable funding might invest in teacher coaching, advanced coursework, or new SEL platforms, while a high-poverty district may focus its limited funds on basic staffing or interventions mandated by the state.

Local control also adds complexity. Each district can set its own procurement thresholds, approval processes, and preferences. For example, in one district, a principal may be able to purchase a $5,000 curriculum supplement on the spot, while in another that same purchase might require approval from the central office, board review, or inclusion on an approved vendor list. Or a district with a change-resistant school board might shy away from programs with a perceived "political" edge while another, with more progressive leadership, might actively seek out equity-focused or culturally responsive offerings.

What this all means for nonprofits is that sales strategies must be highly localized. A great product won't sell if it doesn't fit the district's budget, timeline, or political context. Knowing not just *what* you're selling but *where* you're selling—and to whom—is key to getting in the door.

Philanthropy

Philanthropy has long been a catalyst for innovation in education, from funding charter schools in the 1990s to underwriting tutoring initiatives, edtech tools, and AI pilots today.

While they rarely pay for core operations in schools, philanthropy and personal donors are often the launch pad for nonprofits, especially when there's potential for broader systems change. They can fund your early R&D; help you run pilot programs; and support the development of new offerings before the market is ready to pay. But to scale your impact, and sustain your work long term, you'll need a revenue model that doesn't rely solely on grants.

Foundations are increasingly asking: "What happens when our funding runs out?" Nonprofits that can articulate a credible, mission-aligned revenue strategy that is grounded in a real understanding of how the education market works are far more likely to earn long-term investment and trust.

Who makes the decisions?

Selling to schools is rarely a one-call close. Below are the key players you will need to know:

District administrators

Understanding the district office is essential to any school-facing sales strategy. These leaders shape priorities, control budgets, and manage procurement. While their titles may differ from one district to the next, their influence is consistent.

Superintendents

Superintendents set the district's vision and overall direction, often balancing competing pressures from school boards, state mandates, and community stakeholders. But they're also stretched impossibly thin, managing everything from staffing crises to media inquiries to fiscal oversight.

For sales, this means superintendents may be the final sign-off, but rarely the first stop. You're unlikely to get meaningful time with them unless your solution is directly tied to a top-line district priority or introduced to them by a trusted intermediary. The key is to respect their role as gatekeeper while focusing your early efforts on the staff who vet solutions more deeply.

Chief Academic Officers (CAOS) / Curriculum Directors

These leaders are the intellectual engine behind a district's instructional strategy. They evaluate curriculum, professional learning, and academic interventions, and are often the key decision-makers for products that touch teaching and learning.

You will need to engage these leaders early with evidence of impact, alignment to standards, and clarity around implementation. They're deeply mission-driven, but wary of generic pitches. If you can speak their language and connect your offering to student outcomes, they can become your strongest advocates. But if your message feels vague or overly commercial, you'll lose them fast.

Directors of Technology / Chief Technology Officers

These leaders manage edtech platforms, device ecosystems, data systems, and infrastructure. If your solution requires integration with existing tech (like single sign-on, rostering, or LMS compatibility), they are essential.

Tech officers will want to know about things like security, compliance (e.g., FERPA, COPPA), and support requirements. Conversations here are often technical, and can slow down a sale if your team isn't prepared. That said, a tech leader who sees your product as clean, secure, and easy to implement can smooth your path across the finish line.

Procurement officers

Procurement staff don't usually evaluate your product's merit, but they are the gatekeepers when it comes to compliance. They handle vendor registration, contract negotiation, and purchasing thresholds.

Interactions with procurement officers can feel transactional, but they are critical. Delays in procurement can derail a deal even after everyone else has said yes. So, get ahead of the process: understand what paperwork is needed, be ready with insurance and tax documentation, and ask early about approval timelines.

School principals

Principals and assistant principals often make (or heavily influence) purchasing decisions, especially for professional learning, supplemental curriculum, school climate initiatives, and other building-level priorities. Their authority varies widely by district. In some systems, principals control discretionary budgets and can approve purchases up to a certain dollar amount without central office involvement. In others, they may have little formal purchasing power, but still play a key role in shaping what gets prioritized or piloted.

Engaging school leaders can be a smart early move, particularly if your offering solves a clear building-level challenge, like increasing student engagement, supporting English learners, or boosting teacher retention. They're often more accessible than district administrators, and their enthusiasm can spark interest further up the chain.

However, principals are also navigating immense daily demands: staffing shortages, behavior incidents, parent complaints, and compliance requirements. If your outreach feels like "one more thing" on an already crowded plate, it may be ignored. On the flip side, if you offer something that addresses a pain point they're feeling right now—and you can make adoption easy—they can become powerful champions who advocate for your work at the district level.

Bottom line: Don't underestimate school leaders. They may not always write the check, but they often open the door.

Teachers

Teachers are frontline users and trusted advisors, and their buy-in is critical for implementation success—even if they don't hold the purse strings.

A program might check every box for a district administrator, but if teachers find it clunky, irrelevant, or burdensome, it's unlikely to gain traction in the classroom. That's why smart organizations design with teachers in mind and involve them early in the sales and adoption process, even if they aren't the ones signing the contracts.

Teachers can influence purchasing in several key ways:

- They often serve on selection committees for new curriculum or instructional tools.

- They provide feedback during pilots or trials, which can make or break a final decision.

- Their enthusiasm—or resistance—can sway school leaders and district administrators alike.

So, how should you engage them? It's a balancing act. If you focus *only* on teachers, you risk stalling at the classroom level without ever getting budget approval. But if you skip them entirely and pitch only to decision-makers, you may win the sale but lose the implementation.

The best approach? Devise a two-lane strategy:

- For **decision-makers**, lead with outcomes, alignment to priorities, and cost-effectiveness.

- For **teachers**, lead with usability, relevance, and impact on students.

Offer teachers demo access, highlight teacher testimonials, and co-design features or training materials with real classroom input. If teachers become advocates, their support can accelerate adoption, deepen usage, and improve renewal rates.

Parents and communities

While families are not direct buyers in most K–12 contexts, they can exert significant influence over purchasing decisions, especially in high-profile or politically sensitive areas. Their voices show up in school board meetings, media coverage, and local elections, all of which can shape what district leaders feel empowered (or pressured) to buy.

For example:

- A district considering a new SEL curriculum might abandon the effort if a vocal group of parents frames it as "political" or misaligned with community values. Conversely, a coalition of parents advocating for better bilingual education can push a district to adopt a new curriculum or professional development focused on multilingual learners.

- In some communities, parents' complaints about excessive testing have led districts to invest in more formative, instructionally aligned assessment tools. In others, rising concern about reading scores has fueled demand for "science of reading"–aligned programs, with families asking school boards to act.

For nonprofits, this dynamic can cut both ways. If your offering aligns with a widely felt community need—especially one that parents are organizing around—it can create grassroots momentum that opens doors. But if your work touches a politically contested area (e.g., race, identity, mental health, sex education), you'll need to be prepared for scrutiny, and ready to support district partners in managing the public narrative.

In short: families don't write the check, but they can influence who does. If you're not attuned to local context, even the best solutions can meet with unexpected resistance.

Policymakers

At the state level, legislators, governors, and state education agencies can change everything with a single law or policy directive. These changes often ripple quickly through districts, creating sudden urgency—and funding—for certain kinds of solutions.

For example:

- A **statewide literacy mandate** might require that all K-3 teachers be trained in the "science of reading." Practically overnight, districts begin seeking PD providers, aligned curriculum, and student screeners that meet new state criteria.

- A **new accountability policy** could place increased emphasis on growth measures, prompting districts to adopt interim assessments or data analytics platforms to track progress.

- A **governor's initiative on career and technical education** (CTE) might come with dedicated grant funding, opening the door for nonprofits that support college and career readiness.

- A **change to school funding formulas** could shift dollars toward rural or high-poverty districts, influencing where and how providers target their outreach.

For mission-driven organizations, these policy shifts can create windows of opportunity—but only if you're paying attention. Being policy-aware allows you to position your offerings as timely, compliant, and helpful in navigating new mandates. It also means your sales and program teams can anticipate demand and support districts as they adapt to change, rather than react after the fact.

In education, policy creates the current, and organizations that align with that flow tend to move faster and farther.

So, once we've considered all the factors above, we can definitively state that if you're attempting to sell a product, service, or idea to the K–12 education market, you are operating in a system that is:

- **Fragmented and decentralized**—there's no single playbook, and every district or school type works a little differently.

- **Driven by multiple funding sources**, each with its own rules and timelines.

- **Populated by many decision-makers and influencers**—there's rarely just one person to convince.

- **Shaped by broader forces**, including philanthropy, politics, and state or federal policy trends.

At first glance, this may seem like a daunting set of challenges—and it is. But here's the good news: *When you understand the system, you can start to work with it, not against it.* Clarity brings power. Instead of guessing, you'll be able to plan. Instead of chasing, you'll begin to lead.

When you understand who holds the purse strings, who has the influence, and how dollars flow through the system, you're not operating on hope. You're building relationships, earning trust, and creating the conditions for real impact—and real sustainability.

The key thing to remember here is that the most successful nonprofits treat education leaders not just as customers, but as *collaborators*. They don't just "sell"—they solve real problems, at the right time, in the right way. That's the mindset this book will help you cultivate.

In the chapters to come, we'll explore how to align your offerings to real needs, build trust with decision-makers, and structure your sales and marketing efforts in ways that feel authentic, strategic, and sustainable. Because once you understand the system, the next step is learning how to move through it with confidence and purpose.

REFLECTION QUESTIONS

1   What kind of product, service, or support does your orga-
    nization offer, and where does it fit within common school
    or district priorities (e.g., curriculum, assessment, profes-
    sional learning, edtech)?

2   Where in the system do you tend to engage most—dis-
    tricts, schools, after-school providers, or families?

3   Who are the key stakeholders you interact with during
    your sales or partnership conversations, and who might
    be missing from that picture? (e.g., buyers, users, influ-
    encers, gatekeepers like procurement or IT?)

4   What local, state, or federal policies could shape demand
    for your work, *or* create barriers to adoption? (e.g., Are
    there literacy mandates, SEL restrictions, or funding shifts
    you should track?)

5   What role has philanthropy played in helping you get trac-
    tion, and what would it take to translate that early support
    into a sustainable revenue stream?

2

YOUR THEORY OF CHANGE
The Foundation of
Organizational Stability

MALIK HADN'T BEEN sleeping much. It wasn't just the stress of running a nonprofit during budget season, though that would've been enough in itself—it was the deeper, more existential pressure building in the background.

His organization, CareerBridge, had spent the past six years helping high schools build more equitable CTE pathways, especially for students of color in under-resourced communities. The model was working: they'd helped launch new programs in over a dozen districts, supported hundreds of students in earning industry-recognized credentials, and partnered with state education agencies on best-practice toolkits.

But now, the grants that had fueled that early growth were drying up. Malik's team was smaller than it had been last year. A key district partner had paused its contract due to budget cuts. And while the mission still burned hot, the bank account did not.

So, when his board chair gently suggested that they explore earned revenue—perhaps packaging their CTE coaching into a fee-for-service model for districts—Malik flinched. He understood the logic, but, emotionally, it felt like a betrayal of CareerBridge's mission.

"We're not a business," he confided to a friend that night. "We're here to fight for equity, not chase clients."

But two weeks later, with payroll looming and options dwindling, Malik gave in to reality. He sketched out a basic offering; created a one-pager that, to him, felt more like a sales sheet than a mission statement; and had an exploratory call with a district innovation lead in a neighboring state. That's when something unexpected happened.

The innovation lead was *excited*. She said she'd been looking for just this kind of support. "We've got ESSER dollars left this year," she said. "Can you send over a scope of work?"

Malik hung up and sat at his desk, stunned. This wasn't selling out. This was showing up. This was a district that was willing to pay for the kind of change CareerBridge existed to deliver.

As, nervous but determined, he started building his first revenue plan, he came to a realization: the path to sustainability didn't have to come at the expense of his mission. In fact, it might be the very thing that would finally allow that mission to reach more schools, more educators, and more students.

THIS IS THE KIND OF "eureka" moment the MissionMarket Model is designed to guide you toward: that point when mission-driven changemaking and earned revenue, which are so often seen as opposing forces, begin to align. Malik had reached that inflection point because he was already clear on his mission. That clarity didn't just anchor him—it pointed him forward.

Before you dive into sales—mapping customer segments, setting prices, writing pitch decks—you need to take one foundational step: you have to get crystal clear on *why your organization exists in the first place.*

Not your tagline. Not your boilerplate. I mean the real *why*—the change you're here to create, the problem you exist to solve.

Remember, *earned revenue is just a tool.* Whether it amplifies your mission or pulls you off course depends on how grounded you are in that mission from the start. When you are, revenue builds resilience and expands your reach. When you're not, even well-meaning strategies can lead you astray.

At EdSolutions, we've worked with hundreds of nonprofit leaders who were navigating this exact same tension. Many fear that pursuing revenue will compromise their purpose— and who can blame them? For decades, the nonprofit sector has been fed a false dichotomy: that business thinking and social good don't mix. That money, in and of itself, is suspect.

But here's the truth: money isn't the enemy of your mission. Misalignment is.

That's where your **Sustainability Plan** comes in. This is your organization's blueprint for long-term financial health and lasting mission impact. It's not a business plan in disguise: it's a mission-centered tool that clarifies your purpose, connects it to measurable outcomes, and helps you design strategies—including funding strategies—that make your work last. It helps you *operationalize* your mission, not dilute it.

As you'll recall from the introductory chapter of this book, the ultimate purpose of the ten-step MissionMarket Model is to help you create that Sustainability Plan for your organization. Gaining an understanding of the education market, as we covered in Chapter 1, is the precondition for that plan. Now, in this chapter, we're going to cover the plan's true foundation: your *theory of change.*

NOTE TO READERS

As with Chapter 1, many readers may already be well acquainted with the concept of a theory of change. If that's you, feel free to skim this chapter, or skip ahead to Chapter 3.

But, if you're perhaps starting to feel like your current theory of change may be more of a hopeful wish than a clear map, the step-by-step process below can help you clarify where it may be falling short, and provide guidance on how you can strengthen and sharpen it.

From mission to map: Your theory of change

Every nonprofit has a mission statement. Some are bold, some are brief, some are poetic. Perhaps yours sounds something like:

- "To ensure that every child is able to read by third grade."
- "To close opportunity gaps for multilingual learners."
- "To build a future where every student graduates career-ready."

These statements are important; they declare what you care about. But they don't explain how you'll make that caring matter.

This is where your theory of change comes in. It tells the story of how your work leads to the change you seek. It spells out:

a) the long-term outcome you want to achieve,

b) the key changes that must happen along the way,

c) the activities you're doing to make those changes happen, and

d) the assumptions you're making about how your work creates impact.

And, in addition to being your roadmap from bold intention to real-world results, your theory of change is also the compass for your Sustainability Plan. It helps you:

- identify who your work is for (your beneficiaries and your paying customers),

- clarify which outcomes matter most (shaping your value proposition),

- determine which services you offer (informing your revenue model), and

- understand what kind of capital you need (illuminating where earned revenue fits in).

A strong theory of change isn't just a strategic tool—it's a shield against mission drift and a guide for strategic growth.

So, how do we go about building one?

Building your theory of change

Step 1: Start with the end in mind

Before you can build a sustainable business model, you need to be crystal clear on the long-term change your organization is working to create—not just the inspiring vision, but the specific outcome you want to achieve in the real world.

That might sound obvious, since most nonprofits are born from a deep sense of purpose. But, as we've seen time and again at EdSolutions, this is one of the most common places where even experienced leaders get stuck. It's one thing to care about "educational equity," but it's another to define, in measurable terms, what success actually looks like.

The fundamental question you need to ask yourself is: What specific, observable result are you trying to make true in the world—and for whom?

A vague answer to that question might sound like:

- "Close the opportunity gap."
- "Increase equity in education."
- "Support student success."

Now, all of those are well-intentioned, but none of them give your team a clear target to aim for. A specific, long-term goal sounds more like:

- "Double the percentage of multilingual learners reading on grade level by third grade in our partner districts."

- "Ensure 80% of high school students in our programs graduate with an industry-recognized credential."

- "Increase postsecondary enrollment by 25% for students from low-income backgrounds in urban districts."

These aren't just more, they're useful. They give your team a destination to design toward, and a future result to measure their progress against.

Don't worry about the perfect wording at this point—you'll have plenty of opportunities to refine it, over time. The goal right now is simply to name what success really means for your organization. Because once you know where you're going, everything else—your activities, your partnerships, even your pricing—starts to fall into place.

ACTION STEP
DESCRIBE YOUR LONG-TERM GOAL

Try to write your long-term goal in one sentence. Who is it for? What will change? How will you know?

Step 2: Identify key outcomes along the way

Once you've named your destination, the next challenge is figuring out how you'll get there. That's where outcomes come in—not just the final goal, but the smaller shifts that signal progress along the way. These early indicators help you course-correct, celebrate wins before the finish line, and build a revenue strategy that reflects the real value you create. And, when it comes to earned revenue, they clarify what your customers are actually buying—not just the activity you deliver, but the results that activity helps produce.

A common pitfall here is that organizations often leap straight from activities to long-term impact, or confuse outcomes with outputs. What is the difference between these two?

- "Trained 100 teachers" is an output—it tells you what happened, but not what changed.

- "Teachers use culturally responsive reading strategies" is an outcome—it shows how your work is making a difference.

Let's say your long-term goal is to increase postsecondary enrollment for students from low-income backgrounds. Your intermediate outcomes might include:

- High school counselors shifting to asset-based advising models

- Students reporting greater confidence in postsecondary planning

- Increases in FAFSA and application completion rates

These aren't just metrics for your dashboard, they're clues. They reveal where real change is happening, as well as where your offerings might need to focus—for example, you might realize that your programming skips a critical early shift, or that your success hinges on something you've treated as peripheral. Whatever you may end up discovering, this is often the moment when your strategy sharpens most—and when your theory of change gets real.

Just like with your long-term goal, specificity matters here. Don't stop at, "Improve teacher practice." Ask: Improve how? To what end? How will we know?

These outcomes become your design criteria. They guide your programs, they anchor your value proposition, and they shape the story you will tell funders and customers— not just about what you hope to achieve, but about what's already starting to change.

ACTION STEP
DEFINE THE FIRST SIGNS OF IMPACT

Identify two to four concrete shifts that would signal your work is making progress. Start with the next six to eighteen months—what outcomes will you need to realize during that time to put your long-term goal within reach?

Step 3: Identify your core activities

With your destination set and your outcomes mapped, it's time to focus on what you actually do.

This might sound straightforward—most nonprofit leaders can list their programs and services in a heartbeat. But this step is about more than naming what you offer: it's about intentionally tracing each activity back to the outcomes it's designed to drive. That's the difference between a theory of change that reads like a brochure, and one that works like a compass.

Your core activities are the building blocks of your impact: they're things like coaching sessions, workshops, curriculum development, technical assistance, policy briefs, or direct service. These are what your customers and funders see, but in your theory of change, they're more than services you provide—they're tools for driving the change you're seeking to make.

This means that, if your activities aren't clearly connected to the outcomes you identified in Step 2, your strategy is fragmented. Or, if they are connected but you haven't fully articulated how they're connected, your impact story will feel fuzzy to your team, your board, and your partners.

This step is also where your revenue strategy starts to come into focus. Once you're clear on which activities drive change, you can begin to ask key questions like:

- Which of these activities create value customers will pay for?

- Which can be standardized, bundled, or scaled?

- Which are essential to our mission, and may need to be subsidized?

To illustrate this in an example, let's say that your desired outcome is that teachers use culturally responsive literacy practices. If that's the case, then your core activities might include:

- Facilitating a year-long coaching program for instructional coaches

- Delivering in-person workshops aligned to the district's ELA framework

- Creating a self-paced professional learning module in English and Spanish

Each of these connects directly to the outcome, and could plausibly be part of a fee-for-service offering. But none of them started purely as products—they are all responses to what must be true for impact to happen.

This is the mindset shift we're aiming for. Your work isn't defined by what you already offer, it's defined by what your outcomes require. Once you adopt that approach, your programming sharpens, your sales pitch clarifies, and your Sustainability Plan becomes far more strategic.

If, upon comparing your activities to your outcomes, you find that there is a mismatch between them, that's okay. This is your chance to adjust so that you can let go of those activities that no longer serve the mission, or redesign them so they do. Your theory of change isn't just a reflection of the past. It's a tool to help you do better.

Because the best nonprofit strategies don't just showcase your work: they align your work with your purpose, and give you a path to grow with both integrity and clarity.

ACTION STEP
CLARIFY THE PURPOSE AND
PROOF BEHIND YOUR PROGRAMS

Look at your current list of programs or services. For each one, ask:

a) What outcome is this activity designed to achieve?

b) What evidence do we have that it actually does?

c) Are there activities we should drop—or new ones we should add—to better advance our goals?

Step 4: Articulate your assumptions

Every strategy rests on a set of beliefs—about how the world works, how your partners will act, and how your services will lead to change. This step is about surfacing those assumptions: naming those things that must be true for your activities to produce the outcomes you're aiming for.

Think of these assumptions as the invisible threads holding your theory together. They're the conditions you're counting on, consciously or not, for your work to succeed.

For example:

- "We assume schools will make time in their PD calendar for our workshops."

- "We assume families will attend literacy nights if they're offered in their home language."

- "We assume district leaders will retain enough staff to carry the work forward after coaching."

Beliefs such as these aren't inherently unreasonable; indeed, they're often rooted in direct experience. But every such belief carries an inherent risk that, should conditions change, they may no longer be true. And if you don't name and plan for those risks, your strategy may be more vulnerable than you realize.

And when earned revenue enters the picture, these assumptions become even more important. You might assume district leaders will pay for coaching; that funders will renew their support; that schools will stay on board if one enthusiastic principal leaves. But those are assumptions, not guarantees—and they shape how you price, staff, and communicate your value.

That's why this step matters. When you articulate your assumptions, you can then ask yourself important questions like: How likely is this to hold true? What will we do if it doesn't? Should we adjust our approach, or invest in making that condition more likely?

This isn't just good planning, it's responsible leadership. Many nonprofit strategies fail not because the mission was flawed, but because unspoken assumptions didn't hold up.

So, how do you identify these assumptions that you've based your strategy upon?

First, go back to the step above and look again at the connections you drew between your activities and your outcomes. Then, ask yourself questions like:

- What has to go right for this to work?
- What needs to be in place for our programs to succeed?
- What are we relying on that's outside our control?

Once you've named your assumptions, you can start designing around them. Maybe that means adding an onboarding step to build partner buy-in; or creating a contingency plan for lost funding; or even rethinking a part of your model that rests on a shaky premise.

The goal here isn't to eliminate every risk (which wouldn't be possible anyway): it's to lead with your eyes open. Because strategy isn't only about what you do, it's also about what you believe has to happen, and how prepared you are if it doesn't.

ACTION STEP
PRESSURE-TEST YOUR ASSUMPTIONS

Once you've identified your assumptions, ask yourself the following questions:

a) What are the top two to three things you're counting on that haven't been tested or guaranteed?

b) Where is your strategy most vulnerable to outside forces?

c) What could you do now to learn more—or reduce the risk—before moving forward?

Step 5: Draw the connections

Now that you've defined your long-term goal, mapped the outcomes that lead toward it, named the core activities that drive those outcomes, and surfaced the assumptions holding it all together, it's time to take a step back so that you can see the whole system you've been shaping. Your activities, outcomes, and assumptions aren't isolated elements, but part of a cause-and-effect story. Mapping the connections helps you (and your team, board, funders, and partners) see how your work fits together.

This is where your theory of change becomes real. It's where you draw the line from what you do to what changes—and, ultimately, to why it matters.

You don't need a polished logic model, just clarity. A whiteboard, sticky notes, a basic flow chart—anything that helps you answer the key questions:

- How do our activities lead to our short- and medium-term outcomes?

- How do those outcomes build toward our long-term goal?

- Where are our assumptions showing up, and how do they influence our likelihood of success?

This kind of visual thinking is important. Once you can see the full picture, you can start spotting things you couldn't before: gaps in logic, redundant steps, or surprising insights about where your real leverage lies. You might notice outcomes that depend on activities you're not yet offering, or assumptions that hinge on factors outside your control. Those aren't failures, they're insights. They give you a chance to refine your model, evolve your programming, or forge new partnerships.

And, strategically, this is the step that unlocks alignment. Once your team sees how their work ladders up to something bigger, they can make better decisions. Once funders understand the logic behind your impact, they're more likely to invest. Once prospective customers see how your offering leads to the results they care about, your sales conversations become easier—and your revenue strategy gets stronger.

Let's take Malik and CareerBridge, who we met at the beginning of this chapter, as an example. CareerBridge supports equitable CTE pathways for students of color in under-resourced districts. Here's how that theory of change might look in three common formats:

1) Column-based flow—this format reads left to right, and is great for showing clear cause-and-effect relationships

Figure 2.1.1: From Activities to Impact – A Sample Theory of Change Flow

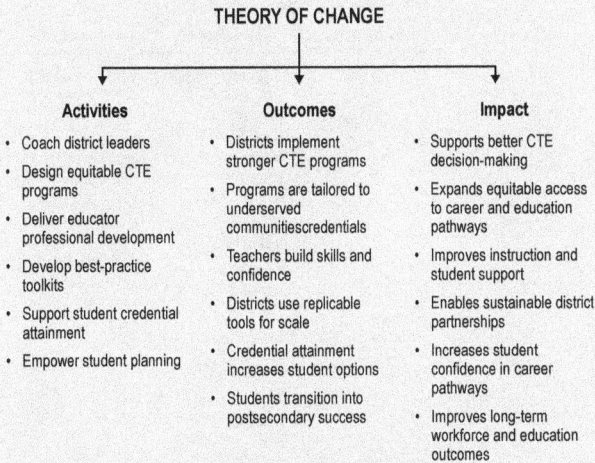

THEORY OF CHANGE

Activities	Outcomes	Impact
• Coach district leaders	• Districts implement stronger CTE programs	• Supports better CTE decision-making
• Design equitable CTE programs	• Programs are tailored to underserved communitiescredentials	• Expands equitable access to career and education pathways
• Deliver educator professional development	• Teachers build skills and confidence	• Improves instruction and student support
• Develop best-practice toolkits	• Districts use replicable tools for scale	• Enables sustainable district partnerships
• Support student credential attainment	• Credential attainment increases student options	• Increases student confidence in career pathways
• Empower student planning	• Students transition into postsecondary success	• Improves long-term workforce and education outcomes

2) Circular system map—a circular map shows how the elements reinforce each other over time

Figure 2.1.2: From Activities to Impact – Activities Flow and Outcomes

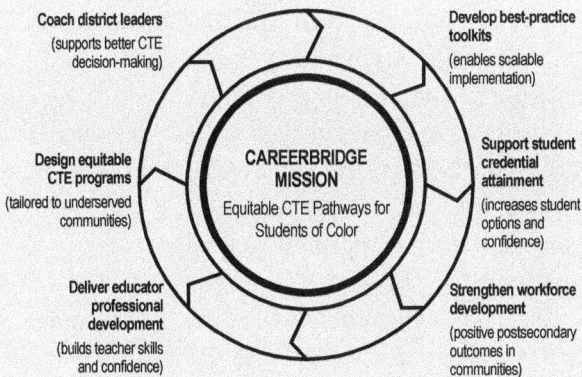

Coach district leaders
(supports better CTE decision-making)

Develop best-practice toolkits
(enables scalable implementation)

Design equitable CTE programs
(tailored to underserved communities)

CAREERBRIDGE MISSION
Equitable CTE Pathways for Students of Color

Support student credential attainment
(increases student options and confidence)

Deliver educator professional development
(builds teacher skills and confidence)

Strengthen workforce development
(positive postsecondary outcomes in communities)

3) Simple board slide—if you were presenting to your board, a one-slide diagram could work like this:

Figure 2.1.3: From Activities to Impact – CareerBridge Theory of Change

CAREERBRIDGE THEORY OF CHANGE

Our Mission	How We Do It	What Changes	Ultimate Impact
• "Build equitable career and technical education pathways for students of color in under-resourced communities."	• Coaching district leaders • Designing equitable CTE programs • Delivering educator professional development • Developing best-practice toolkits • Helping students earn industry-recognized credentials	• Districts implement high-quality CTE pathways • Programs are tailored to underserved communities • Teachers gain skills and confidence • Districts use replicable tools for scale • Credential attainment increases student options • Students report greater confidence in career planning	• Equitable access to career and technical education • Sustainable, equity-focused district partnerships • Improved postsecondary and workforce outcomes for historically underserved students

If you've ever sat in a funder meeting struggling to articulate your impact, or stared at a blank page while drafting a fee-for-service proposal, you'll already know that a revenue strategy without mission clarity is just noise. That's why building your theory of change is always the starting line. It gives your revenue strategy shape; it clarifies what you're offering, who it serves, and what changes as a result; and it helps you see where value is created so you can decide, with confidence, which parts of your work can and should be monetized.

Here's how the elements of your theory of change connect to drive your revenue strategy:

- Your long-term goal shapes the kinds of outcomes your customers care about.

- Your intermediate outcomes become proof points (and key selling points) in conversations with funders or district partners.

- Your core activities are what you'll eventually package and price. When you know how they drive change, you can describe them with confidence.

- Your assumptions help you anticipate risk so you can decide when to guarantee outcomes, when to pilot first, and when to partner instead of sell.

We all know that selling in the nonprofit space can feel uncomfortable: it can stir fears about mission drift, inequity, or losing your identity. But when your offerings are rooted in the outcomes you exist to achieve, those fears start to fade. Because now, you're not just "selling a service," you're scaling a solution. You're inviting schools, districts, or partners to participate in the impact you're already committed to creating.

When you've done this work, everything that follows gets easier—and smarter. Because:

- You'll know which customers are aligned with your mission because they care about the same outcomes.

- You'll know what to say in a pitch because you understand the journey your offering supports.

- You'll have a pricing rationale that's rooted in the results you deliver.

- You'll have the clarity to say no to opportunities that don't fit.

- And most importantly, your team will be able to scale without compromising what makes your work meaningful, because everyone will be rowing in the same direction.

Now that you've grounded your work in purpose, it's time to explore how to connect that purpose to real-world demand. In the next chapter, we'll dig into identifying your customers—who they are, what they need, and how to prioritize them as you build your organization's Sustainability Plan.

REFLECTION QUESTIONS

1   What long-term change is your organization trying to create?
2   What outcomes tell you you're making progress?
3   How do your current programs or offerings align with those outcomes?
4   What assumptions or external factors shape your ability to succeed?
5   How will this theory of change shape your revenue strategy?

3

UNDERSTANDING YOUR CUSTOMERS
Stop Preaching, Start Listening

ON A GRAY TUESDAY morning in October, Jamal sat across from his board chair with a familiar tightness in his chest. The quarterly numbers were in, and they weren't good.

The product his team had built—a beautifully designed, research-backed digital toolkit to help teachers differentiate instruction—wasn't selling. Again.

"We've got some uptake in a few schools," Jamal said, trying to sound optimistic. "Teachers who use it love it. They're saying it's finally helping them reach their struggling students."

His board chair nodded gently. "But principals aren't buying it," she replied.

She was right. Despite months of outreach, demos, and pilot offers, school leaders kept passing. "No budget," some said; "Too many other initiatives," said others. One principal had told Jamal, flat out: "We don't have time to figure out new tools. We're buried."

Jamal walked back to his office frustrated. He didn't understand. He'd spent fifteen years in classrooms and central offices, and he knew the system was broken. He'd seen how one-size-fits-all instruction failed kids—especially the ones from the communities he cared about most. So he had started his nonprofit with a bold vision of bringing better, equity-focused tools to teachers. He had poured everything into the solution: grants, sleepless nights, even his personal savings. He'd assumed that if he built something good— really good—people would find it, use it, and spread the word. But that simply wasn't happening.

In his gut, Jamal still believed that school leaders should be buying what he was selling, and that they were wrong to ignore it. He believed that it was his job to open their eyes, to convince them—to convert them. "I'm not selling," he'd told a friend once. "I'm doing mission work."

But over time, Jamal's language had shifted. He found himself talking more about pipeline, less about purpose; worrying about burn rate, not just impact. And his team had started asking hard questions: "Who is our ideal customer?" "Why aren't they picking up the phone?" and, most pointedly, "Why are we chasing teachers when the buyers are district administrators?"

That last one particularly stung. Jamal had built the whole product around the end user—teachers—because he believed in empowering them. But teachers didn't hold the purse strings, districts did. And district leaders had different priorities: data reporting, integration with other platforms, PD hours. These were things that Jamal hadn't focused on— things that, frankly, he had thought didn't matter in relation to his own mission.

Now, sitting at his desk, Jamal began to realize something he hadn't wanted to admit: he'd fallen in love with his solution, not his customer.

That was the moment something cracked open. Maybe, he thought, it was time to stop trying to convert people, and start trying to understand them.

JAMAL'S JOURNEY IS one that many education nonprofit leaders have taken: starting with a strong mission, building a promising solution, and then running headfirst into a wall of "no."

The hard truth is, good ideas don't always win. No matter how thoughtful, well-designed, or urgently needed they are, these ideas can get stuck, passed over, or undervalued—not because they aren't worthy, but because they don't line up with the priorities of the people who actually make the decisions.

But when you truly understand your customers—their goals, their constraints, the pressures they face—you stop spinning your wheels and start connecting. You move from frustrated missionary to strategic partner—from trying to convince to learning how to serve. And that shift can change everything.

The third step in the MissionMarket Model is all about getting you laser focused on the individuals and institutions who are most likely to say "yes" to you—not someday, but soon. It will help show you that, rather than chasing every opportunity, you need to zero in on the right-fit customers for your product or service—the ones who both align with your mission, and will fuel your sustainability.

We've laid some of the groundwork for this step in the previous chapters. First, we surveyed the structure of the U.S. K-12 system, identifying how money moves around it, who makes the decisions regarding it, and why timing, politics, and local context matter. We began to see the system not as a monolith, but as a network of overlapping forces that ultimately determine what gets adopted, funded, and scaled.

Then, we clarified your theory of change—the end goal of the impact you hope to make, the intermediate outcomes you're working toward, the levers you believe will move those outcomes most effectively, and the assumptions upon which all this work is based. You got clear on your role in the system, and why it matters.

This chapter, then, is where your system knowledge meets your strategy. It's where your mission meets the market, where you go from preaching to listening. It's about shifting the question from:

"How do we get them to care about what we do?"

to

"What do they care about, and how does our work help them?"

In the pages ahead, we're going to walk through how to:

- understand the different kinds of "customers" in education—from the people who benefit from your work to those who fund it,

- create simple, actionable customer profiles that inform your outreach strategy and,

- prioritize those right-fit customers—the districts, schools, or funders—that align best with your mission and business model.

However, before we can reach those right-fit customers, we first need to understand how the term "customer" really works in this world—because in education, it's not always obvious, and it's rarely just one person.

Who's who in the education system: Know your stakeholders

In the for-profit world, a customer is usually the person who pays, clean and simple; in education, not so much. In this space, you might design services for students; rely on teachers to implement them; get paid by a district; and report results to a foundation.

So, the question is: Who (or which one) is your customer?

The answer may sound a little unhelpful at first blush: It depends on what decisions you're trying to influence. Because to navigate this landscape, you need to think in terms of roles, not just titles.

Titles can sometimes be deceiving. Depending on the district or education sector in which you're operating, someone with "coordinator" in their title might wield major influence, while a "director" might have little real authority.

Roles, on the other hand, reveal what someone actually does in the buying journey. For instance, are they the person using your program? Approving the budget? Shaping opinions behind the scenes?

Once you understand the role each person you're dealing with plays—not just what's printed on their business card—you can start to tailor your approach more effectively.

Most education nonprofits have at least four different kinds of stakeholders to consider:

1 **The Beneficiary.** These are the people your organization exists to serve—students, families, educators, or communities. They are your why. You design with them in mind, measure success based on their outcomes, and

stay grounded in their needs. But here's the catch: they often don't hold purchasing power.

2   **The User.** The users are the ones who interact with your offering every day. They're the teachers who deliver your curriculum, the counselors who run your SEL programs, the coaches who lead your PD. They can be your greatest champions, or your biggest barrier to entry. Because if the user doesn't believe in your work, it can be a tough road ahead for you.

3   **The Influencer.** These folks might not control the budget, but they hold sway. They're trusted principals, well-regarded instructional coaches, PTA leaders, or even policy advocates. If they love your work, they can open doors. If they're skeptical, good luck.

4   **The Buyer.** This is the person who writes the check. They approve the budget, sign the contract, and take on the risk. Often, it's a central office leader: a chief academic officer, director of curriculum, or foundation program officer. They are the gatekeepers of your growth.

While all the stakeholders in the list above factor in to the decision-making process, all too often, mission-driven organizations get fixated on the beneficiary and user levels. That's completely understandable, because that's where their heart is—that's who they want to help.

But, when it comes to earned revenue—that is, the sustainability of your mission—the buyer is ultimately the one who has the power to say "yes." Understanding who that is—and what makes them tick—is essential, because even the most beloved program won't last if the buyer doesn't believe it's worth paying for.

ACTION STEP
LEARN FROM THE
PEOPLE WHO SAID "YES"

Write down the names of:

a) One user who really champions your work

b) One buyer who has written the check

Now ask yourself:

- What did each of these people care most about?

- How were their priorities different?

How to find (and focus on) your right-fit customers

Now that we know who we're dealing with in theory, it's time to start planning how to strategically reach out to them in practice—with a clear, step-by-step path to helping you identify, and prioritize, your real customers.

1. Start with what you know

Before you go chasing new leads or building slick pitch decks, take a moment to ask yourself: "Who are we actually serving right now?"

This is your customer audit. Think of it like laying out all your district and partner relationships on the table. What kinds of organizations are they? Big city districts? Rural charters? Statewide nonprofits? What do they ask you for? What makes the relationship work—or not work?

You don't need a complex system or a three-day retreat to do this. You can start by grabbing a teammate, opening a Google Doc, and asking, "Which districts or partners have we loved working with, and why?" That alone can start to reveal patterns you hadn't seen before.

ACTION STEP
REFLECT ON THE RELATIONSHIPS
THAT WORKED

Pull up your calendar, CRM, or just a sticky note. List three past partners or customers you have loved working with.

Now ask yourself:

- What type of organization were they?
- What made the work flow?
- What impact did you create together?

2. Spot the patterns

Once you've identified who you're working with, the next step is to group them. This, to borrow a bit of corporate-speak, is segmenting—which really just means organizing your customers in ways that can help you make smarter decisions.

Let's say you've worked with five districts this year. Three were rural, and they leaned on you to help stretch their ESSER funding. One was a big urban district, which was focused on culturally responsive PD. The fifth was a nimble charter network looking to revamp their ELA curriculum fast. Those are three different segments right there, each with distinct needs, timelines, and constraints.

When you group customers like this, patterns start to emerge. You'll start to notice where things flow easily, where you've gained traction, and where opportunities might be waiting, if you just approached them a little differently.

3. Prioritize what matters most

Once you can clearly visualize your customer segments, you can begin to prioritize them—because the fact is, not all customers are created equal. Some may be beautifully aligned with your mission and ready to move. Others might mean well, but take forever to make decisions, or require so much handholding that the work becomes unsustainable.

Your goal here is to figure out who your ideal customers are—the ones who see the value in what you do, have the means to pay for it, and make the kind of progress that reminds you why you started this work in the first place.

That can feel like a lot to figure out, especially if you've been saying "yes" to whatever comes your way just to keep the lights on. But it doesn't have to be a mystery. Start by looking back at your past projects and asking, "Which ones felt great? Where did we deliver strong impact, build trust, and see potential for more?"

4. Sketch out your ideal customer

Once you know the kinds of organizations you want to work with, it helps to bring them to life. This is where customer personas come in. This doesn't mean that you're inventing your ideal customers out of thin air, but rather distilling your ideal customer from the types of people you've already worked with—the ones you wish you could clone.

Picture someone like Tanisha, an assistant superintendent juggling a big equity push, high staff turnover, and board pressure to improve literacy scores. She doesn't need more noise: she needs a partner who listens, understands her context, and helps her move the needle. Or maybe it's Rodrigo, a nonprofit program lead who's trying to reimagine summer learning with a shoestring budget and a tight timeline.

When you really understand what these folks care about—what keeps them up at night, what success looks like for them—you stop writing generic emails and start creating things that actually resonate. Your proposals land. Your pricing makes sense. And your solutions feel tailored, even when they're standardized.

ACTION STEP
CREATE YOUR
CUSTOMER PERSONA

Picture your favorite district partner. Answer the following questions about them:

- What's their name and title?
- What is their biggest pain point?
- What kind of pressure are they under right now?

Take a few minutes to answer those simple questions. Congratulations—you've just drafted your first customer persona!

5. Factor your customer profiles into your overall strategy

Once you've completed all of the work above, you don't want to let those valuable insights sit on a shelf and gather dust: they should feed directly into your Sustainability Plan, your sales strategy, even your program design. Who are your top-priority customer segments? What do they need? How does all this align with your mission and your theory of change?

ACTION STEP
TRANSLATE CUSTOMER SEGMENTS
INTO STRATEGIC ACTION

List your top two or three customer segments, and one insight you've learned about each. This becomes the foundation for your marketing and sales strategy.

USERS & BUYERS—
COMMON PITFALLS TO AVOID

- Equating end users with paying customers. A teacher may love your tool, but a district leader approves the budget. Know who holds the decision-making power.

- Targeting too broadly. "School systems" is not a segment. Be specific. The more focused you are, the more effective you'll be.

- Skipping the research. You are not your customer. Even if you were once in their shoes, things change. Assumptions are easy to make, and often wrong. Talk to your customers. Ask questions. Listen hard.

When you've completed the work in this chapter, you'll have taken a big step forward. You've stepped into the shoes of your customers, and identified the difference between the people who use your work and the people who pay for it. You've mapped the landscape, identified your ideal partners, and started listening to them about what they actually need, not just what you want to give them.

This is a powerful shift in perspective, because once you stop trying to sell to everyone and start focusing on the right people, everything changes. Your outreach becomes more strategic. Your time becomes more valuable. Your work starts to feel less like a grind, and more like a conversation with people who actually want to be part of what you're building. You've begun to connect your mission and theory of change with the actual people who can help bring it to life—by piloting your work, funding your programs, scaling your solutions, or advocating for your approach.

Now that you know who you're trying to reach, it's time to dig into how you reach them.

In the next chapter, we'll draw on all the work you've just done—mapping out your customer segments, determining their priorities, assessing their pain points—in order to articulate your value proposition: that is, how to describe your work in a way that truly resonates with the customers you're trying to serve by speaking to their real needs, and in doing so sets you apart from all the other "solutions" out there. You'll also be able to begin populating the next section of your Sustainability Plan, translating your insights about your ideal customer into messaging that lands and relationships that last.

REFLECTION QUESTIONS

1   Who are the real decision-makers for your solution? Have you been talking to them, or around them?

2   Where have you had the most traction in the past, and why?

3   What assumptions have you been making about your customers? Which ones need to be tested or challenged?

4   Which of your current partners align most closely with your theory of change, and what makes those partnerships work?

5   What are the implications of your ideal-customer profile for your team, your time, and your outreach strategy?

4

DEFINING YOUR
VALUE PROPOSITION
Why They Should Choose You

CARLOS LEANED BACK in his chair, frustration etched across his face. Across from him sat Amanda, the superintendent of Pine Hill school district, her expression polite yet distant.

"Carlos," she said gently, "I understand your passion. But I still don't clearly see what makes your math program different from the others we've tried."

Carlos felt the sting of her words, but he also knew they were fair. He'd heard similar responses countless times.

His nonprofit, EquaLearn, was born from a deep conviction that middle school math could be accessible and engaging for every student, particularly those who have been historically underserved. But despite years of refining his supplemental intervention products, he struggled to explain why a district should choose EquaLearn.

"We help students feel confident about math," Carlos offered, immediately hearing the vagueness in his words. "Our approach is holistic—we incorporate mindset, motivation, and foundational skills."

Amanda nodded patiently. "But what does that mean practically, Carlos? How exactly does your approach boost achievement better than other solutions?"

Carlos paused as he mentally scrambled to formulate an answer to Amanda's question, cycling through a laundry list of anecdotes, research findings, and program features—none of which felt compelling or cohesive.

"Let me get back to you," he said quietly, embarrassment creeping in.

Replaying the conversation in his head later that evening, Carlos finally landed on the crux of his problem. He needed to move beyond explaining what he had built, and instead speak to what it solved. It was time to stop leading with what excited him about his service, and start speaking to why it would matter for them. Because unless he could learn how to communicate EquaLearn's distinctive value—what made it the best option on the table, setting it apart from its competitors—he would continue to miss chances to make a meaningful impact.

MOST NONPROFIT LEADERS aren't taught how to talk about their work like salespeople. And in many ways, that's a good thing: your focus has been on service, not self-promotion.

But when it comes to earned revenue, clarity isn't optional. If your potential customers can't quickly grasp what you offer, why it matters, and how it compares to their alternatives, they won't move forward with you.

In the previous chapter, we explored the importance of listening to your customers so that you could understand what their needs were. In the next step of the MissionMarket Model, we're going to cover how you can clearly, concisely, and convincingly communicate to your customers the way that your product or service will fulfill those needs—what is known as a value proposition.

A strong value proposition helps you:

- differentiate yourself from others in the field,
- sharpen your offerings to better meet customer needs,
- win contracts, grants, or fee-for-service engagements, and
- stay focused on the work that drives impact.

Your value proposition also contributes to your core mission by helping your team stay aligned. Because when everyone—from program staff to grant writers—knows how to describe your value, your message becomes more consistent, your brand becomes stronger, and your opportunities grow.

How to craft a value proposition that actually lands

While "value proposition" sounds like another one of those corporate-speak terms that can give nonprofit folks the shivers, at its core, it's really just your answer to a simple, powerful question: "Why would someone choose to work with us, especially when there are so many options out there?"

What distinguishes your value proposition from your mission statement and your theory of change is that it isn't about what you want to say: it's about what your customers need to hear—and believe—so that they can feel confident saying yes. Your value proposition isn't a slogan, it's a promise to your customer—a clear, specific reason why your work matters to them.

So, how do we go about designing your value proposition for maximum impact?

1. Start with your customers, not your programs

Before you jump into crafting your value proposition, return to the work you did earlier in this book—especially the part where you mapped out your customer segments and their top needs. Your value proposition should always begin with your customers' world, not your offerings.

It might help to revisit a few basic questions:

- Who are your highest-priority audiences right now?

- What are they struggling with?

- How do those struggles connect directly to your mission and theory of change?

This quick reflection helps keep you focused on delivering real value, not just listing features. If you skip this step, you risk building a message that's all about you, instead of one that makes someone else feel seen.

ACTION STEP
START WITH WHAT MATTERS
MOST TO YOUR AUDIENCE

- Write a sentence beginning with: "Our customers want…"

- Follow that with a second sentence that completes this phrase: "So we help them by…"

This simple two-sentence exercise helps you cut through the noise and focus on what your customers actually care about. It ensures your value proposition starts with their problems—not just your programs.

2. Define what makes you different

Once you've established what your customers need, it's time to turn the spotlight inward: What makes you the right partner for them?

This isn't about puffing yourself up—it's simply being honest, and specific, about the ways your organization is uniquely equipped to help. Ask yourself questions like:

- What outcomes do we help people achieve?
- What's different about how we do it?
- What do we offer that others don't, or can't?

Maybe you have a proven coaching model that's been refined over years. Maybe your tutors are all trained former teachers. Maybe your organization has deep, long-term relationships in a specific region, or your materials are explicitly designed with cultural responsiveness in mind. The answers you come up with could cover a whole range of possibilities, but whatever they are, they will be unique to you.

You can look to outside evidence for this definition as well. Think about feedback you've received, outcomes you've measured, or moments when a district leader said, "You really get us." These are all clues to your unique value.

If it helps, imagine explaining what makes you different from a peer over lunch, rather than trying to articulate it to a funder or write it up for a pitch deck. This can help you keep it honest and human.

ACTION STEP
DEFINE YOUR DIFFERENTIATORS

Jot down three things you consistently hear from partners or funders. Start with:

- "You really helped us..."
- "What makes you different is..."
- "Other orgs we've worked with didn't..."

These are real-world clues to your unique value. Make sure to capture them before they fade.

3. Survey the landscape

One of the most revealing parts of the value-proposition process (and, ironically, one that many organizations overlook) is looking around to see who else is offering products or services that could be regarded as similar to yours. Even if you've never thought of yourself as having "competitors," your potential customers definitely see you as only one within a whole landscape of options. They're weighing you against other organizations, in-house solutions, or even just doing nothing at all.

Imagine a leader at an education nonprofit who finally has a quiet afternoon to review the websites of a few of their peer organizations. As they scan the pages, they notice something unsettling: "Wait... our coaching model? Our language about equity and outcomes? Other groups are saying almost the exact same things."

It's easy to panic in that moment, but here's the opportunity—what sets you apart may not be the what, but the how and for whom. Maybe your team brings deep expertise in multilingual learner support. Maybe you specialize in high-poverty rural districts, or you've got a proven track record with state-funded pilots.

That kind of clarity can change the game. You're not trying to outshine everyone—you're trying to find your distinct lane, especially for the customers who need what you offer most.

You don't need to spend hours on market research. Just answer a few essential questions: Who else offers something similar? What are they claiming? And where do you shine in comparison, especially for the kinds of customers you care about?

ACTION STEP
SCAN THE LANDSCAPE

Identify two or three peer organizations you respect (or compete with). Take a look at their websites or pitch decks. Then, ask yourself:

- What are they emphasizing in their descriptions of their products or services?

- Which kinds of customers do they seem to be targeting?

- How does your work stand apart from them? (Identify three to four key differentiators.)

4. Craft your value proposition statement

Now comes the fun part—bringing all those insights together into your value proposition statement. This is your clear, confident answer to "Why you?"

A strong value proposition says:

- Who you serve
- What problem you solve
- How you solve it uniquely
- What outcomes your partners can expect

For example:

- "We help school districts close literacy gaps by providing evidence-based tutoring aligned to their curriculum. Unlike other providers, our tutors are trained former teachers, and our model integrates seamlessly into the school day."

- "We help foundations and districts make smarter investments by providing rapid-turnaround research grounded in practitioner voice. Unlike traditional academic firms, we deliver insights in weeks, not months—and always with clear, actionable next steps."

- "We support school systems in retaining high-need students by delivering trauma-informed after-school programming rooted in youth voice and community partnerships. Unlike traditional programs, we co-design experiences with students and train school-based staff to carry them forward long after the grant ends."

Your value proposition doesn't need to be flashy, just clear and direct. You can tailor it slightly for different audiences (funders, school leaders, intermediaries, etc.), but the core message should stay consistent.

Once you've drafted your value proposition statement, add it to your Sustainability Plan, right alongside your customer insights and competitor notes. In this way, it becomes a touchstone for your whole organization. It keeps your proposals sharp, makes your messaging stronger, and helps your whole team stay aligned on what you're offering and why it matters.

> **ACTION STEP**
> **DRAFT AND TEST YOUR**
> **VALUE PROPOSITION**
>
> Try writing your value proposition in one sentence using this formula:
>
> > "We help [target customer] achieve [desired outcome] by [your unique approach]."
>
> Say it out loud. If it feels clunky or vague, revise until it feels natural and clear.

How to tailor your value proposition for different audiences (without losing your message)

It can be tempting, after doing all that work to devise your value proposition statement, to then treat it like a one-size-fits-all tagline. But your target audiences are not all the same, which means that your language shouldn't be, either.

A school superintendent, a program officer at a foundation, and a community-based nonprofit partner may care about the same student outcomes, but they'll approach the problem from different angles, with different goals, constraints, and language. This means that your value proposition might need to flex. The key is to tailor how you deliver your message without changing what you're saying. Think of your value proposition as if it were a solidly constructed house: that sturdy foundation will stay the same, but the way you arrange your front porch might change depending on who's walking up to the door.

For example, let's say your core value proposition is:

> *"We help small and rural school districts build stronger reading outcomes for multilingual learners by providing in-class coaching led by local educators. Unlike other providers, we embed our support within the school day, using materials that reflect students' home languages and cultures."*

Now imagine you're speaking to three different audiences:

- A **district CAO** might need to hear:

  > *"This model is designed for districts like yours—short on staff, long on need. We integrate into your schedule and build your internal capacity, not your workload."*

- A **funder** might respond more to:

  > *"Our approach closes opportunity gaps in rural districts where most models won't go, and it works with the staff already on the ground. We've seen reading gains of twelve points in a single semester."*

- A **community partner** might resonate with:

  > *"We prioritize home language, cultural pride, and educator voice, because kids learn best when the adults in the room see them fully."*

In each of the examples above, the value proposition doesn't change, but the lens shifts. When you tailor your message correctly, you'll be speaking the languages of your different target audiences, while staying firmly rooted in your own voice.

As you scale your outreach, take the time to craft a few differently tailored versions of your message for your highest-priority audiences. This won't just help with sales, it will also make your proposals, websites, and presentations more resonant and relevant.

To see another example of this tailoring process in action, let's return to the story of Carlos from the beginning of this chapter:

A few weeks after that tough meeting with Amanda, Carlos sat down with his team and worked through the questions in this chapter. They pulled up feedback from districts they'd worked with, reviewed results from their most successful pilots, and got honest about what made EquaLearn *different*, not just better.

The final value proposition they landed on wasn't flashy, but it was clear:

> "We help middle schools boost math outcomes for multilingual learners by combining targeted intervention with identity-affirming supports. Unlike other programs, EquaLearn integrates academic skills with language development and student-led goal setting—so students don't just catch up, they lean in."

Carlos started using this new language in conversations and proposals. At first, it felt a little awkward, but he noticed something almost immediately: district leaders leaned in. Instead of asking him to "clarify," they asked follow-up questions. One district even said, "This is exactly what we've been trying to find."

Within a month, EquaLearn had landed two new pilots and was in early talks for a regional partnership. The biggest shift, though, was internal. Carlos no longer felt like he was defending his work: he was *inviting* people into it, with clarity, confidence, and purpose.

ACTION STEP
FLEX YOUR MESSAGE

Try tailoring your value proposition for two of your target audiences:

- What would a **district leader** want to hear?
- What would a **funder** want to hear?
- What would a **community partner** want to hear?

Remember, in each case your core message will stay the same, but the angle you take will shift. If you can look at your tailored version and still recognize your original value proposition underneath, you're in good shape. If it starts sounding like an entirely different organization, you may have flexed your message a little too far.

YOUR VALUE PROPOSITION—
COMMON PITFALLS TO AVOID

- Being **too generic.** If your value statement could apply to dozens of organizations, it's not specific enough.

- Leading with *features* instead of *benefits.* Customers don't care how your engine works—they care where it takes them.

- Ignoring **competitors.** Your customers are comparing options. You should be too.

You've just built one of the most important pieces of your revenue strategy: a clear, compelling articulation of your value. You've moved from fuzzy passion to focused promise;

from listing features to speaking outcomes. You now have language that can guide proposals, funder meetings, pitch decks, and even how your team talks about your work in everyday conversations.

That kind of clarity doesn't just win contracts, it builds momentum. And, when paired with the right revenue model, it becomes the foundation of a financially sustainable, impact-driven organization. So, in the next chapter, we'll move on from that foundation to ask that all-important question: How exactly will you get paid?

We'll walk through the most common revenue models for education nonprofits, show you how to evaluate which ones fit your work, and help you move from scattered revenue to a structure that actually supports your growth. Because a strong value proposition is only as powerful as the business model that backs it up.

REFLECTION QUESTIONS

1   Can you describe your value in one sentence, without using jargon?

2   What makes your approach truly different, not just slightly better?

3   What do your customers consistently say they appreciate most?

4   Where do you lose deals, and why?

5   How well does your value proposition connect back to your mission and theory of change?

5

DEVELOPING YOUR
REVENUE MODEL
How You'll Get Paid—
and Stay Sustainable

WHEN ALONDRA LAUNCHED ReadingRoots, she felt like everything had finally clicked into place. As a literacy coach for over a decade in a large, multilingual district, she had seen firsthand how many promising classroom interventions never quite reached the place where they mattered most: students' homes. Too often, parents were an afterthought; or, worse, seen as the barrier, rather than the solution.

With ReadingRoots, Alondra flipped that script entirely. She built a model centered on empowering parents with offerings like bilingual literacy trainings, culturally responsive book bundles, and personalized coaching sessions. Teachers and principals raved about the improved home—school connection. Families loved it, and kids were thriving.

Two years ago, Alondra's vision resonated deeply with the BrightPath Foundation, a major philanthropic player whose stated mission was clear: improving literacy outcomes for underserved students. They called ReadingRoots "exactly what we've been looking for." They applauded her approach, celebrated early results, and funded a two-year pilot. For a while, Alondra felt like the darling of the foundation. She'd found her champion.

But now, two years later, something had shifted. BrightPath's program officer was now politely supportive, but less enthusiastic. This was because the foundation's strategic priorities had quietly evolved: they were shifting away from family engagement, and beginning to focus on larger-scale technology programs. ReadingRoots was no longer the shiny new thing, and Alondra could feel it.

As she prepared to present at BrightPath's annual grantee convening, Alondra felt a familiar wave of frustration rising. "You wanted this model," she thought, "You told me this was exactly what the field needed." But she knew the reality was more complicated: she'd built a beautiful solution, but hadn't figured out how to sustain it beyond philanthropy. She'd approached districts repeatedly, but the response was always the same: "We love what you're doing, but we don't really have budget lines for parent programs. Could you maybe come back next year?"

With BrightPath's enthusiasm waning and district budgets closed off, Alondra felt stuck. ReadingRoots was clearly working; everyone said so. But delivering immense value wasn't enough. She needed a plan to ensure that value could continue.

While Alondra didn't have a term for it yet, what she was missing was a *revenue model*—which, simply put, is a way to connect the value she was providing to resources that could help sustain and scale it.

A REVENUE MODEL is your blueprint for how your organization generates income from the products or services you offer. Without a clear revenue model, even the most impactful programs struggle to sustain their impact over time, precisely because the education landscape is complex: budgets are tight, priorities shift, and the path from "great idea" to "sustainable program" can feel like a maze. A strong revenue model gives you the clarity, confidence, and control to navigate that maze. It connects your impact with the funding that enables you to continue delivering results, year after year.

In this chapter, we'll use this simple yet powerful framework to explore different types of revenue models, determine which ones fit your organization best, and show you how to build a practical, sustainable strategy of your own. By the end, you won't just have a clearer understanding of what a revenue model is—you'll see the possibilities, the opportunities and, most importantly, the pathways to financial sustainability and greater impact that are stretching out right in front of you.

The three building blocks of a revenue model

To design an effective revenue model, it helps to break it down into three clear, practical components. Let's return to Alondra and her nonprofit, ReadingRoots, to illustrate how each of these components plays out.

1. What you offer

Your offering is your core product or service—the heart of your organization's value. Clearly defining what you offer helps customers understand precisely how you deliver value and what they're paying for.

Alondra's offering was ReadingRoots' innovative literacy program— as per above, bilingual literacy trainings, culturally responsive book bundles, and personalized parent coaching sessions.

2. Who pays for it

Identifying the right customer—that is, who can and will pay for your product or service—is critical. Clarity about who pays helps focus your outreach, messaging, and pricing strategies.

> *Alondra initially targeted philanthropic foundations, but was then faced with pressure to diversify. Other potential payers for her ReadingRoots offering might include school districts, government agencies, or even individual families.*

3. How they pay

This component addresses the actual payment structure for your offering. For example, do your customers pay per session (fee-for-service)? Do they subscribe annually? Do they license your curriculum?

> *Alondra's current challenge was that her primary customers—foundations—were becoming unreliable long-term payers as their priorities shifted. Exploring different payment structures could help her build a more sustainable path forward.*

ACTION STEP
IDENTIFY YOUR REVENUE-MODEL BUILDING BLOCKS

Write down the current building blocks of your revenue strategy below. If your answers feel a little vague or incomplete at this point, don't worry—this gives you a useful starting point.

- What are we offering?
- Who's paying for it (or could be)?
- How do they pay?

Common revenue models in the K-12 sector

By now, you've mapped out the three building blocks of a revenue model: what you offer, who pays, and how they pay.

These building blocks can be combined in many creative ways, but not all combinations are equally likely. In practice, the "what you offer" block tends to serve as the anchor, because it shapes your cost structure and delivery model. That, in turn, heavily influences how you charge. From there, your strategy for "who pays" becomes a lever you can pull, depending on your mission, customer capacity, and funding landscape.

This is why most education nonprofits ultimately gravitate toward one of three revenue model types:

1 Service-based
2 Product-based
3 Hybrid

Each reflects a common configuration of the building blocks—a pattern that balances mission alignment with financial sustainability. Let's look at each in turn.

1. Service-based

What it is: This model is anchored in "what you offer"—direct services such as coaching, professional development, student programs, or technical assistance. These offerings tend to have *high variable (marginal) costs*, because your team has to show up—live, in person, or online—to deliver them. As a result, the natural "how they pay" structure here is *fee-for-service*, where schools or districts pay for each engagement, session, or contract.

The "who pays" building block can vary. Often it's the district or school itself. In some cases, philanthropy funds early pilots or subsidizes services in lower-resourced contexts. In others, a cross-subsidized model allows affluent schools to pay full price so that underserved schools can receive discounted or free access.

Why it works: This model fits comfortably into school and district budgets. It works best when your impact is closely tied to live delivery and human relationships.

Example: *Alondra could reposition ReadingRoots as a profes-sional development and family engagement service paid for directly by school districts through annual service contracts. Each contract would be priced to reflect real delivery costs, including prep time, coaching, and materials.*

2. Product-based

What it is: This model is built around a codified, replicable product, such as curriculum materials, digital tools, diagnos-tic assessments, or online courses. These offerings usually have *high fixed costs* (to design and build them) but *low marginal costs*, meaning you can serve more users without significantly increasing your expenses. That makes *subscrip-tion or licensing* the most common "how they pay" structure.

The "who pays" block depends on the context. Districts and schools are common buyers, especially when prod-ucts align to instructional priorities and funding streams like Title III or Perkins. In some cases, families might pay directly (e.g., for enrichment or home learning tools). In oth-ers, philanthropy might underwrite the product for a specific population.

Why it works: Product-based models support scalability and predictable revenue. They're especially effective when the offering is content-rich, low-touch, and easy to implement with minimal support.

Example: *If ReadingRoots codified its literacy approach into a digital toolkit—with videos, family guides, and printable resources—it could offer it to districts as a $5,000/year license, or directly to families via a low-cost monthly subscription.*

3. Hybrid

What it is: This model combines elements of both services and products—offering, for example, a curriculum or platform bundled with coaching, training, or implementation support. Hybrid models allow nonprofits to deliver more comprehensive value and meet customers where they are. But they also require careful planning: the mix of *fixed and variable costs* means you need to be clear about what's included, what's optional, and how each element is priced.

The "how they pay" block often involves a base price (for the product) with optional add-ons (for support services), or bundled packages sold at a single rate. The "who pays" side can flex: for example, a district might cover the product while philanthropy funds the implementation support, or vice versa.

Why it works: Hybrid models can be powerful because they pair scale with impact. But they only work when you price based on actual delivery costs and structure your offerings in a way that avoids confusion or scope creep.

Example: *ReadingRoots could offer a monthly subscription of take-home literacy kits for families, and sell companion coaching packages to schools that want to build teacher-family partnerships. One part is scalable; the other deepens impact.*

Putting it all together

The three revenue models above aren't rigid categories; rather, they are common combinations of the three building blocks we introduced earlier.

MODEL TYPE	WHAT YOU OFFER	HOW THEY PAY	WHO PAYS (CAN VARY)
SERVICE-BASED	Coaching, PD, TA	Fee-for-service	Districts, philanthropy, cross-subsidy
PRODUCT-BASED	Curriculum, tools, platforms	License, subscription	Districts, schools, families, funders
HYBRID	Product + support services	Bundle, base + add-on	Mixed: district, philanthropy, families

Think of "what you offer" as the foundation: it drives your cost structure and, therefore, your pricing model. From there, you can choose who pays: direct customers, underwriters, or a blend. The key is not to memorize models, but to design the configuration that fits your work, your economics, and your audience.

How to develop your revenue model

Here's where we start moving from theory into practice—where we take those three current building blocks of your revenue model, and look at them in new ways in order to unlock new paths toward sustainability.

1. Set your revenue objectives

Start by clarifying what you're trying to achieve financially and strategically. Is your priority growth, stability, expanding equity, or achieving greater mission alignment? Knowing your objective helps you pick the right model.

For Alondra, achieving financial stability and reducing dependency on foundation funding was key.

ACTION STEP
WHAT ARE YOU SOLVING FOR?

From the list below, circle the outcome you're most focused on:

- Stability
- Growth
- Diversification
- Equity
- Alignment with mission
- Other

Now, based on your answer to the above, fill in the blanks in this sentence:

> *"Our revenue model needs to help us* [insert priority] *by* [how you'll do it]*."*

2. Diagnose your current revenue reality

Reflect honestly on your current revenue streams. Where is your funding coming from right now? How stable or predictable is it? Understanding your current reality helps identify strengths to build on and gaps to address.

For Alondra, almost all the funding for ReadingRoots was coming from a single foundation, which proved to be risky when that organization's priorities shifted.

ACTION STEP
MAP YOUR CURRENT REVENUE MIX

List out each of your current revenue sources—whether that's philanthropy, earned income, government contracts, or something else. For each one, jot down:

- The **percentage of your total budget** it represents
- How **predictable** it is (e.g., one-time grant vs. renewable contract)
- Any **risks or dependencies** (e.g., tied to a single funder, ending soon, connected to a key relationship)

Then ask yourself:

> If one of these went away tomorrow, what would happen?

This exercise can be uncomfortable—but it's the first step toward building a stronger, more resilient model.

3. Explore your revenue model options

Return to the three revenue-model building blocks you identified earlier: "what you offer," "who pays," and "how they pay." Now, brainstorm two to three alternative possibilities for each one.

- For "what you offer," could you adapt your current program into a new format—e.g., a digital toolkit, a condensed workshop series, or a tiered coaching package?

- For "who pays," are there additional customer types you haven't engaged yet—e.g., schools, districts, families, government agencies, or corporate sponsors?

- For "how they pay," could you shift from one-time contracts to ongoing subscriptions, or create bundled pricing
for multiple services?

Once you've generated a list of options, start mixing and
matching across the categories to explore new combinations.

*As we saw with Alondra, testing different configurations—like
district-paid service contracts, philanthropy-supported pilots, or
family subscriptions—can reveal fresh pathways that align with
both mission and sustainability.*

ACTION STEP
REMIX YOUR REVENUE MODEL

Grab a blank sheet of paper and draw three columns:

- What **we could offer** (e.g., workshop series, digital toolkit,
coaching bundle)

- Who **might pay** (e.g., districts, families, funders, employers)

- How **they might pay** (e.g., license, fee-for-service, subscription, pilot grant)

Now try combining different pieces across the columns. What
new configurations emerge? Don't judge them yet—just generate possibilities. Try at least **five combinations**, even if some
feel like a stretch.

This remixing process can spark creative pathways you hav-
en't considered—and surface models that balance mission and
money in new ways.

4. Evaluate and prioritize your best-fit models

Consider practical criteria: ease of implementation, potential scalability, alignment with your mission, and customer willingness to pay. Create a simple rubric to rank your ideas.

For Alondra, partnering with districts offered clear alignment, while subscription models required deeper market testing.

ACTION STEP
SCORE YOUR REVENUE
MODEL OPTIONS

Pick two or three of the revenue models you generated in the last step. Now rate each one using the following criteria (1 = low, 5 = high):

- **Mission Alignment**—How well does this model support your core purpose?

- **Ease of Implementation**—Can you get it up and running without major new capacity?

- **Scalability**—Could this model grow to serve more people over time?

- **Customer Willingness to Pay**—How likely is it that your target payer will actually pay for this?

Add up the scores for each model. Which one comes out on top? Which ones might be worth revisiting later?

You don't need perfect answers—just a clear starting point for informed decision-making.

5. Test and refine your model

Once you've identified your best-fit revenue model(s), it's time to take it out into the real world. Start small: pilot your chosen revenue model with a targeted customer segment. Collect feedback, measure success, and adjust based on real-world data.

In the case of ReadingRoots, Alondra might pilot a small-scale district partnership or a limited family subscription model first, learning and iterating before scaling up.

ACTION STEP
PICK A PATHWAY TO PROTOTYPE

Which of the three common models below do you think most closely aligns with your offering, and how you want your organization to evolve?

- Service-Based Revenue Model
- Product-Based Revenue Model
- Hybrid Revenue Model

Once you've made your choice, take a moment to reflect: Why this model? What makes it feel like a good fit for your mission, your team, and the communities you serve? Writing down your reasoning can sharpen your thinking—and help you communicate your direction to funders, partners, and your board.

FINANCIAL TERMS YOU NEED TO KNOW

Financial vocabulary can seem intimidating, but it doesn't have to be. Here's a quick rundown of some key terms you'll likely encounter:

- **Earned revenue:** Income generated directly from your products or services, not from donations or grants.

- **Recurring revenue:** Predictable, steady income from subscriptions, annual renewals, or ongoing contracts.

- **Margin:** The difference between what it costs you to deliver your product or service and what you charge for it. Higher margins usually mean greater sustainability.

- **Scalability:** Your ability to expand your reach and impact without significantly increasing your costs.

- **Cross-subsidy:** Charging full prices to customers who can afford it to subsidize discounted services for those who can't.

At this stage in the MissionMarket Model, you've successfully clarified your customer segments; crafted your value proposition; and explored revenue models that match your mission. You've taken your first major steps toward building a more financially sustainable, impact-driven organization.

In the next chapter, we're going to shift from strategy to visibility. Having a great value proposition and a sustainable revenue model won't matter a bit if the people who need you most never hear about you. How do you get in front of the right people, with the right message, at the right time? How do you help your mission find its right-fit customers? In short: How do you generate *leads*?

REFLECTION QUESTIONS

1   Which revenue model(s) are we using today? Are they intentional, or inherited?

2   Which parts of our model feel strong? Which parts feel fragile?

3   Where could we evolve our revenue model, by layering, packaging, or piloting something new?

4   Does our current model allow us to *invest* in our mission, or just *maintain* it?

5   What could a more sustainable model unlock for our team, our partners, and the communities we serve?

6

FINDING YOUR PEOPLE
Marketing in the K–12 World

LEILA, THE CHIEF academic officer for Brookdale Unified School District, stared at her inbox, which was flashing a daunting "317 unread" message in bold red. A quick glance at the subject lines told her everything she needed to know:

"Boost Math Scores Today!"
"Next-Gen Learning for All Students!"
"Personalized Learning at Scale!"
"Quick chat this week?"

It was pretty much the same story with her voicemail: fourteen new messages since yesterday, mostly from vendors she didn't know, pitching solutions she hadn't asked for. And her LinkedIn DMs? Don't even ask.

It's not that Leila was shirking her responsibilities, or that she didn't care about improving learning conditions for her students. In fact, she cared deeply.

Brookdale had seen a surge in multi-language learners (MLLs) over the past three years, and the district's existing math curriculum just wasn't cutting it. Teachers were trying, but the instruction materials simply weren't designed with MLLS in mind. Leila had seen the data and heard from principals: her MLL students were disengaged and falling behind.

She needed a supplemental math program that was rigorous, culturally responsive, and accessible to students learning English—something that didn't just translate word problems, but supported true comprehension. Vendor after vendor came to her claiming that their program "worked for all kids," but when Leila dug deeper (on the rare days she actually had time to do so), very few showed real design features for English learners.

Leila sighed, clicked "Archive All," and moved on to prep for her 3 p.m.

ACROSS THE COUNTRY, Maya sat in the corner of the cramped office of her education nonprofit, NumberBridge, staring at a Google Sheet full of cold outreach attempts. She had founded the organization three years ago to solve the very problem Leila was trying to fix.

Maya and her team had co-designed their math supplement with MLL students and teachers in Title I schools. It used visual modeling, embedded vocabulary supports, and featured native-language scaffolding. Early pilots were promising: students were more confident, teachers reported stronger engagement, and formative data pointed to real growth.

But none of that mattered if no one knew that Number-Bridge's solution existed. And on most days, Maya felt like she was shouting into a void.

NumberBridge couldn't afford to have a booth at every conference, much less create flashy ad campaigns or recruit paid influencers. So Maya and her team had tried emails, social media, even cold calls. But their messages were going into jam-packed inboxes, and their voicemails were getting buried. The CAOs and curriculum directors they most needed to reach had no opportunity to understand their value. NumberBridge was just one more bodiless name in an overstuffed field.

Maya sighed, and refreshed her email one more time. Still nothing.

UNBEKNOWNST TO EITHER of them, Leila and Maya were blindly orbiting around each other—both looking for the same thing, both too overwhelmed or invisible to make the connection.

This story isn't rare. It plays out across the K-12 landscape every day. District leaders are actively looking for better ways to support students. Nonprofits are actively trying to reach them. And yet, again and again, the right people miss each other.

Why does this happen? For one simple reason:

Because even the best-designed program, the most promising intervention, or the most impactful research project won't matter if no one hears about it.

And that's where *marketing* comes in.

Returning to Maya's story above, you can see that she has bought in to the necessity of *selling* NumberBridge's solution. But if you simply jump straight into your sales efforts—cold calling, pitching, emailing decision-makers, and so on—without setting the stage through marketing, it's like walking into a room full of strangers and expecting them to say yes before they even know who you are.

Marketing is how people find you, understand you, and begin to trust you. It's what gets you in the room. Sales is what you do once you're in there.

So, in this chapter, we're going to focus on how to get you through that door and in front of the people who want and need your solution—even if they don't know it yet. We'll show you how to build a marketing and outreach plan that creates traction, not just noise. You'll learn how to choose the right tactics and help the right people find you, before you ever pick up the phone.

You've built the engine. Now let's put it on the road.

How to build a marketing plan that actually generates leads

If you've been in the nonprofit field for a minute, you've likely done some things that could fall under the umbrella of "marketing." Maybe you've posted on LinkedIn a few times, or put together a one-pager you're proud of. But for all too many mission-driven organizations, when it comes to actually getting new leads in the door, these kinds of efforts are often too scattered, intermittent, and variable in tone, message, and approach to be truly effective.

The good news is that you don't need to go out and hire a dedicated marketing team, or become a full-time marketer yourself in order to do this right. As with the previous work we've done in the MissionMarket Model, what you need to do is ground yourself in the core value you have to offer your ideal customers, and build your messaging and marketing plan around that.

As we go through each of the six steps below, we're going to show how Maya implements each of them in order to devise a new, strategic, and effective marketing plan for NumberBridge, so that you can get a clear illustration of how this process works in practice.

1. Reconnect with your audience

Marketing always starts with the "who"—as in, *who* are you actually trying to reach?

The thing to remember at this stage is that, while we've already done work in the previous chapters to identify your relevant customer segments, these are not set in stone. As your programs evolve and your focus sharpens, your target customers might begin to shift, too. Maybe six months ago, you were focused on chief academic officers; now, though, you're seeing more traction with ELL coordinators or state-level program officers.

So, continually check back in on and reassess your *customer personas*. Who are your customers? What do they care about? Where do they hang out, both online and in real life? For example, a district leader buried in emails all day isn't going to see your Instagram post, but she might open a smart, well-timed newsletter—especially if it comes with a free tool or article she can use with her team tomorrow.

This is a good time to revisit the steps we covered in Chapter 3, especially the practice of mapping out decision-makers, influencers, and champions in your space. Use those tools again now, but with an eye toward marketing: Where are these people getting their information? What are they reading? Who are they already listening to?

You don't need to conduct formal research for this: a quick scan of a few sources can go a long way. Try browsing:

- Education Week or The 74 to see what issues your customers are talking about

- LinkedIn to follow superintendents, CAOs, or nonprofit peers in your space

- Council of the Great City Schools to see what large districts are prioritizing

- GovWin or state procurement sites to spot patterns in RFPs and contracts

You might also listen to relevant podcasts, join a few webinars, or review the newsletters your customers likely subscribe to. Even just skimming the headlines can help you pick up on the themes, pressures, and language your audience is responding to.

Now let's see how this step works out for Maya:

Maya starts by revisiting her target customer. She pulls up her notes from past partnerships, scans through email threads, and reflects on who has shown genuine interest in NumberBridge.

It turns out the most promising conversations haven't come from the top-level superintendents she's been chasing, but from Chief Academic Officers and Directors of Multilingual Education—especially in districts with large populations of English learners.

With that in mind, Maya sharpens her ideal-customer profile: she's looking for CAOs in medium-to-large urban districts serving high percentages of multilingual learners, with access to Title I funding and a stated commitment to improving math outcomes. These are the folks who not only need her solution, but have the authority and the resources to act on it.

ACTION STEP
STEP INTO YOUR CUSTOMER'S WORLD

Pick one of your target customer personas (e.g., a CAO or program officer). Ask yourself:

- What newsletters, podcasts, or professional networks would they be tuning into?

    - Make a list of 2 or 3 sources and start reading or listening regularly to stay attuned to what your audience cares about.

- Where do they go for ideas or inspiration?

    - Identify one or two events, communities, or online spaces where you might show up—whether by attending, contributing content, or simply observing.

- What topics are they most likely to click on or engage with right now?

    - Jot down 2 or 3 themes you notice across channels; that's the foundation for your next message or content piece.

2. Refine your message

Once you've homed in on who you're talking to, it's time to focus on *what* you're saying to them.

Your message is what makes someone pause. It's the thing that makes them stop scrolling, open the email, or lean in a little when you're speaking on a panel. A good message doesn't just describe your work, it makes your audience *feel* something. It taps into their real challenges, needs, and desires.

That means it can't just be a plain statement of fact, or, conversely, an emptily grabby catchphrase. Your message needs to be anchored directly in your value proposition: what you do, who it's for, and why it matters.

You've already done this foundational work in the Value Proposition chapter, where you defined the specific problem you solve and the unique way your organization creates value. Here, you're simply translating that internal clarity into language that will resonate with the people you most want to reach.

So, for example, instead of:

> *"We offer instructional coaching for teachers."*

You say:

> *"We help districts keep great teachers by giving them the coaching support they actually want."*

Instead of:

> *"We provide after-school tutoring."*

You say:

> *"We help students who've fallen behind in reading catch up—and stay up—by making tutoring feel like a confidence boost, not a punishment."*

Or, instead of:

> *"We conduct student assessments."*

You say:

> *"We give teachers real-time insights so they can stop guessing and start teaching what students actually need."*

Each of these alternatives still describes the same work as their initial versions, but instead of purely functional (and vague) descriptions, they lead with the outcome, speak to the audience's emotional drivers, and position the solution as something helpful and human.

That's what a truly refined message does: it helps people recognize themselves in your work.

Maya takes a fresh look at NumberBridge's message. She realizes that while her team's original language is accurate, it isn't exactly magnetic. They've focused on features—visual models, vocabulary scaffolding, native-language supports—but haven't clearly articulated the program's benefits.

So, she drafts a new message that leans into outcomes and urgency:

"NumberBridge helps multilingual learners succeed in math by equipping teachers with culturally responsive tools that drive engagement, confidence, and growth—without adding to their workload."

This version passes the test: it's clear, direct, and anchored in what matters most to her audience.

ACTION STEP
PUT THE OUTCOME FIRST

Choose one of the programs, services, or products you offer. Now try to craft a compelling (and truthful) message about it using the formula below:

> "*We help* [audience] *achieve* [outcome] *by* [your unique approach]."

If it feels dry or vague, take another run at it. And conversely, if it feels too cute or "sales-y," go back to the drawing board and refocus on that core value of your offering—the aim here is *clarity*, not cleverness.

3. Build your "funnel":
Determining your marketing objectives

One of the most common mistakes nonprofit teams make is thinking marketing is just about visibility. But visibility alone isn't the goal—you want *movement*. You want to guide people from simply hearing about you, to actually *engaging* with you. In marketing terms, this is often called a "funnel."

A marketing funnel is a simple model that maps the journey a potential customer takes—from first learning you exist, to becoming interested in your work, to deciding whether to engage, and, ideally, becoming a partner or client. It's called a funnel because, just like in real life, you start with many people at the top, and only some of them make it through to the bottom.

Figure 6.1: The Marketing Funnel – Your Customer's Buying Journey

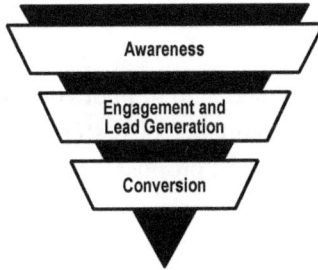

At the top of the funnel, your goal is *awareness*—making sure the right people know you exist.

Examples:

- your organization is featured in a prominent newsletter, or

- you make an appearance on a conference panel, or

- a thought-leadership article from your team is shared on LinkedIn by a trusted peer

In the middle of the funnel, the goal is *engagement and lead generation*—helping those right people better understand what you offer, why it matters, and how they can connect with you more deeply.

Examples:

- a potential customer visits your website, or

- reads an article or guide you've published, or

- signs up for your mailing list

At the bottom of the funnel, the goal is *conversion*—which means moving someone from interest to commitment, such as scheduling a pilot, signing a contract, or agreeing to purchase your solution.

Examples:
- a potential client signs up to pilot your program, or
- schedules a call to finalize next steps, or
- requests a customized proposal to move forward

You don't need to pursue all of these funnel stages at once; in fact, trying to do too much can dilute your efforts and drain your team's energy without delivering results. Instead, it's often more effective to choose one or two marketing objectives to focus on for a defined period of time—say, a quarter or semester.

Which part of the funnel you prioritize should depend on your current needs and context. If most of your target audience still hasn't heard of you—or doesn't really understand what you do—then your focus should be on building awareness. That means showing up in the right spaces, speaking their language, and creating that initial spark of recognition.

But maybe you're in a different position: the right people *do* know who you are, but they aren't reaching out, clicking through, or asking to learn more. In that case, the goal is engagement and lead generation—turning recognition into curiosity and curiosity into action. What content or experience would make them say, "Tell me more"?

Or perhaps you already have leads, but they're stalling out. If you're getting early interest but few decisions, your marketing may be working, but your sales strategy and conversion process need attention. (Don't worry, we'll tackle that head-on in the next chapter.)

Wherever you are, the key is to choose one clear objective that aligns with your current reality. That clarity will help you shape your strategy, pick the right tactics, and focus your limited time and energy where it matters most.

Maya is done with cold outreach. Her new objective is simple: stop chasing leads, and start *attracting* them.

Specifically, she wants to grow her list of warm leads—that is, district leaders who match her target profile and are actively engaging with content in the multilingual learner space. If just a few of those people reach out proactively, it could change everything. Maya knows she needs to shift from interruption to invitation.

ACTION STEP
CHOOSE THE RIGHT FOCUS FOR RIGHT NOW

Every marketing plan should start with a clear objective. Below are three common goals (aligned to the stages of the funnel) to help you pick the one that best fits your current situation:

- **Awareness**—if your target customers don't yet know who you are or what you offer.

- **Engagement & Lead Generation**—if people know your name, but aren't interacting with your content or exploring your offerings.

- **Conversion**—if you're getting warm leads, but they aren't turning into sales or longer-term partnerships.

Reflect on which stage feels most important right now, and let that focus anchor your strategy for the coming months

4. Define your strategy

Here's where we start working out the "how." Your strategy is your game plan—your big-picture approach to how you'll reach your audience and move them through the funnel.

It's not about doing everything, but about choosing a path that connects your goals with your strengths and resources. Your strategy should align with your marketing objective (awareness, engagement and lead generation, or conversion), reflect your organization's brand and mission, and align with the realities of your team's capacity.

Think of it as your throughline: if someone asked, "How are you planning to reach your ideal customers this year?" your strategy is the one- to two-sentence answer you'd give in reply. For example:

- If your objective is **awareness**, your strategy might be: *"We'll build visibility by showing up as thought leaders in the multilingual learner space through blog posts, webinars, and targeted partnerships."*

- If your goal is **engagement and lead generation**, your strategy might be: *"We'll deepen relationships with district leaders by sharing useful, relevant resources that reflect their real challenges and offer practical solutions, and also provide strong calls-to-action to engage more deeply."*

- If your priority is **conversion**, your strategy might be: *"We'll move interested leaders toward commitment by making it easy to pilot our program, sign an agreement, or move into a longer-term partnership."*

A good strategy narrows the field. It doesn't just say what you *could* do, it clarifies what you *won't* do right now. It guides your messaging, your channel choices, and your team's day-to-day efforts.

Maya decides to meet her ideal customers where they already are. So, she and her team start to brainstorm: What conferences, newsletters, or associations do multilingual learning leaders trust? What spaces do they turn to for ideas and inspiration?

One organization keeps coming up: the National Association for Bilingual Education (NABE). It has a large national audience, a focus aligned perfectly with NumberBridge's mission, and regular content features like webinars, blogs, and email roundups.

Maya's team marks NABE as a high-priority channel. If they can get visibility there, they'll likely reach dozens—if not hundreds—of their exact right-fit customers.

5. Devise your tactics

As we covered in the step above, your strategy is your big-picture game plan; your *tactics* are the smaller-scale tools, actions, and initiatives you undertake to put that plan in motion. Think things like blog posts, email campaigns, webinars, events, social media, and so forth—these are the lines of communication by which you look to reach your ideal customers.

The key here is to not try to use that whole arsenal. Start small: pick two to three tactics that align with your audience and your message. For example, if your audience is instructional leaders in mid-sized districts, a well-targeted webinar series and a monthly resource email might do more for you than a dozen random tweets. Finding a way to convert your most loyal customers into advocates will likely do more than any amount of cold calling.

Returning to the funnel model, here are some more ideas for the kinds of tactics you could employ at each of the three stages, drilling down further and further to where you actually get your customers to sign on the dotted line:

- **Awareness**:
  - guest appearances on podcasts
  - SEO-optimized blog posts
  - conference panels

- **Engagement and lead generation**:
  - downloadable guides
  - short video explainers
  - LinkedIn thought-leadership articles and strong CTAs

- **Conversion**:
  - pilot program agreements
  - customized proposals
  - direct outreach to finalize a purchase

Again, the magic here isn't in doing more—it's in doing the right things consistently.

Maya's team springs into action. One staff member researches NABE's editorial guidelines. Another drafts a short blog post called "Five Ways to Support Multilingual Learners in Math," drawing directly from NumberBridge's classroom work. Maya offers to submit the article, and reaches out personally to NABE's content editor, who not only accepts the piece but invites her to speak on an upcoming webinar.

It's a simple, focused tactic—no paid ads, no glitzy campaign, just a useful article in a trusted space, followed by a warm, mission-aligned opportunity to share their story.

ACTION STEP

CHOOSE YOUR TACTICS

Looking at the list of communication channels below, ask your-self: Which feel most natural to you? Which align best with your right-fit customers? Circle two to three of the most applicable options; these are your priorities.

- Email
- LinkedIn
- Webinars
- Podcasts
- Blog posts
- Other:

_____

_____

_____

_____

6. Delegate the work

Even the best marketing plan won't run itself, so here's where you get down to brass tacks. Who on your team will lead the different aspects of your marketing efforts? What's your monthly time and budget commitment? And, crucially, how will you know if it's working?

You don't need a full-time marketing hire to get started on this. Many small nonprofits begin by carving out a few hours a week from someone's existing role, or by rotating marketing responsibilities across the team. The key is to assign clear ownership: Who is drafting the newsletter? Who's following up with webinar attendees? Who's posting to LinkedIn?

Just as important as *who's doing what* is having a shared sense of *whether it's making a difference*. You don't need complex dashboards to get started. Begin by identifying a few simple indicators that connect directly to your marketing goal:

- if your focus is **awareness**, track where and how often your work is showing up (e.g., mentions, shares, conference invitations)

- if it's **engagement and lead generation**, look at open rates, clickthroughs, or direct replies to your outreach

- for **conversion**, track how many prospects are moving from interest to commitment (e.g., agreeing to a pilot program, signing a contract, requesting a proposal)

Keep it simple. You can jot results in a shared spreadsheet or do a quick monthly debrief: *What did we try? What happened? What should we keep, change, or stop?*

In a future chapter, we'll go deeper into how to track your sales pipeline and assess performance over time. For now, your job is to make a clear plan, assign responsibilities, and build the habit of checking in.

Maya sets aside time each week to support the content effort and prep for the webinar. Her teammate manages communications and logistics. When the webinar airs, over 300 bilingual educators and district leaders tune in—including, as fate would have it, Leila, the Director of Multilingual Learning from Brookdale Unified, a mid-sized urban school district with a growing population of English learners, who is looking for a math intervention that better supports her multilingual middle school students.

A couple of days later, Maya receives an email from Leila, which reads simply:

"Really appreciated your presentation—this is exactly the kind of program we've been looking for. Can we schedule time to connect?"

Within a week, Leila's message is followed by email from three other district leaders, all of them wanting to know more about NumberBridge.

Maya's strategy has worked. She hasn't guessed who to chase, and desperately (and indiscriminately) flooded inboxes with outreach efforts that are destined to go unanswered: she's used a focused, thoughtful marketing plan to help the right people find her.

ACTION STEP
DEFINE OWNERSHIP, RESOURCES, AND MARKERS OF SUCCESS

To make an honest appraisal of your situation and resources, answer the following questions:

- Who on our team will own the marketing function?

- What's our time/budget commitment for our marketing efforts?

- How will we be able to determine if those efforts are working, and how often will we review those results?

You don't need to have perfect answers right now. Use this as a reflection prompt to start the conversation, and revisit it as your plan takes shape. Progress here is about clarity, not completion.

Your marketing plan isn't just about making a sale, it's about building a bridge. It connects your organization's work to the people who need it most. It helps them find you, understand you, trust you, and, eventually, reach out.

Remember: there is a CAO, a principal, or any number of other decision-makers out there who need *exactly* what you've built. And when you strategically send out your lines of communication—when you identify *who* your ideal customers are, *where* you are most likely to reach them, and *how* you can best convey your message and value proposition—you are doing *them* a valuable service. You're helping them cut through the noise that bombards them every day, and guide them toward the solution that's right for them. *Your* solution.

Now that we've covered how to reach those ideal customers you're looking for, it's time to learn about what to do once they reach back out to you. This is the stage where marketing hands off the job to *sales*. Great marketing gets you in the room; great selling is what actually moves your mission forward.

In the next chapter, we'll break down every stage of the sales process: the discovery call, the pilot offer, and the art of turning interest into a deal. And, most importantly, we'll discuss how to evolve that initial sale into a real, mission-aligned partnership.

REFLECTION QUESTIONS

1   Where are we currently most discoverable, and where are we invisible?

2   What do our ideal customers most need to hear from us?

3   Which marketing tactics feel most authentic to our voice and audience?

4   Are we generating *interest*, or just sending out *information*?

5   What will we need (people, time, budget) to execute our plan consistently?

7

MAKING THE SALE
How to Convert
Demand into Revenue

JASMINE HAD ALMOST canceled the meeting three times. She told herself that Dr. Martinez, the district leader she was scheduled to speak with, was probably too busy; that she herself wasn't ready; that this wasn't the right moment. But deep down, she knew the real reason she'd tried to avoid this: she didn't want to come off like she was trying to sell something.

Jasmine had spent a decade working in schools before founding her nonprofit, Pathways to Teaching, which helped paraprofessionals become certified teachers. She loved the work; she loved her team. And she had no doubt the model worked: it had already helped over 100 classroom aides transition into full-time teaching roles.

But, when it came to actually selling that model, something in her stomach twisted. She'd been on the receiving end of pushy pitches from edtech companies before, and the last thing she wanted was to sound like a vendor. She wanted to lead with mission, not marketing.

So, when the Zoom call began, Jasmine tried to stay warm and conversational. She shared her story; she asked thoughtful questions about the issues Dr. Martinez was dealing with. But when the opportunity arose to talk about a partnership—or what the district might do next—she hesitated.

"I mean, I don't want to assume anything," she said, waving off Dr. Martinez's direct question about costs. "We're really just trying to be helpful and learn what's going on in the field."

Dr. Martinez smiled. "I appreciate that. Well, keep us posted!"

And so, their call ended—very politely, very sympathetically. And also with no next step, no proposal, and no invitation to follow up.

Jasmine closed her laptop, frustrated with herself. She hadn't pushed. She hadn't pitched. And now, she didn't have a path forward. She'd let her aversion to selling—or rather, her fear of being seen to be selling—get in the way of the valuable solution she was actually *offering*.

BY THIS STAGE of the MissionMarket Model, you've come a long way. You've identified your ideal customers; clarified your value; determined how you'll get paid; and built a marketing plan that helps the right people find you. And now, it's happening: a district leader has filled out your contact form, or a funder has replied to your newsletter, or a colleague has made an intro to a decision-maker, who says to you, "We've been hearing about your work, and would love to talk."

This is the moment that separates awareness from action. It's the moment when someone says, "Tell me more." And you need to be ready for it.

For many nonprofit leaders—especially those in the education sector—the process (and even the notion) of sales can often feel off-puttingly transactional, aggressive, or just plain awkward. But, when it's done well, sales can simply be an extension of that core value your program or service has to offer. It's about listening deeply, offering support, and guiding the right people toward the right solutions. It's the bridge between interest and impact. It's the process that turns curiosity into commitment, and commitment into revenue that fuels your mission.

To be a successful seller doesn't mean you need to be a slick closer. What you need is a mission-aligned, repeatable process for converting leads into partnerships—with clarity, integrity, and confidence. Because you're not "selling" in the traditional sense: you're inviting someone to partner with you in making change.

Figure 7.1: Marketing vs. Sales: Know the Difference

MARKETING		SALES
Creates awareness and interest	>	Converts interest into a deal
Happens before the conversation starts	>	Happens during/after conversations
Broad communications	>	One-on-one engagement

So, in this chapter, we're going to cover how to:

- respond to interest with professionalism and purpose,
- lead discovery conversations that build trust,
- present offers that speak to real needs,
- handle objections without fear, and
- close deals that sustain your work.

How to build a mission-aligned sales process

Step 1: Make your sales process clear and simple

Think of your sales process like a relay race, not a scavenger hunt: each step should hand off smoothly to the next, with a clear direction and no unnecessary detours. The goal is to create a straightforward, intentional sequence that builds trust and momentum.

i)   **Inquiry**—a potential customer reaches out to you through your website, a colleague, or a marketing campaign; maybe they saw your newsletter or attended a webinar. However they found you, they've now raised their hand.

ii) **Discovery**—you schedule a 30–45-minute conversation to learn more about their goals, challenges, and context. Your job here is to *listen*, not pitch.

iii) **Proposal**—based on what you learned in the discovery call, you follow up with a tailored proposal. This might be a one-pager, a slide deck, or a short scope of work that outlines your offering, as well as the outcomes, the timeline, and the cost.

iv) **Decision**—the ball is now in their court. But you're still engaged—answering questions, adjusting the proposal if needed, and making it easy for them to say yes.

v)   **Contract/start**—once they give the green light, you finalize the paperwork and kick off the partnership.

ACTION STEP
WHAT IS YOUR CURRENT SALES JOURNEY?

On a whiteboard or a large sheet of paper, sketch out your current sales process, from first contact to close. Now ask yourself:

- Who does what at each stage?
- What happens at each stage?
- Where does the process feel unclear, inconsistent, or slower than it should be?

Refer to the sample journey above (Inquiry → Discovery → Proposal → Decision → Contract/Start) as a guide. Your process doesn't have to match it exactly, but seeing how your own steps compare to it can help you spot gaps, clarify handoffs, and simplify the path forward.

Step 2: Assign roles and responsibilities

Now let's get specific: who does what?

- Who responds to new inquiries—and how fast?
- Who schedules and leads the discovery call?
- Who drafts and sends the proposal?
- Who follows up if there's no response?

Let's say you're a three-person team. One person could be the designated responder (within forty-eight hours); another could lead the discovery conversation; and a third could draft the proposal. Or maybe it's *all* you, but you still map it out so nothing falls through the cracks. The goal is to make the process feel both seamless for your potential partner, and sustainable for your team.

Here's what that might have looked like for Jasmine at Pathways to Teaching:

After a few scattered follow-ups and missed opportunities, Jasmine decided that her team needed a clearer, more intentional approach. So, she broke down roles and responsibilities by:

- asking her program manager to monitor inbound emails and respond to new inquiries within one business day

- taking the lead on discovery calls herself, since she could speak with credibility and warmth about the organization's story and strategy

- assigning her colleague in operations to handle proposal drafting, using a shared template that they could customize for each opportunity

With those roles clarified (and captured in a quick-reference doc), Jasmine and her team were now able to move faster, follow up more consistently, and make every prospective partner feel well taken care of.

Step 3: Qualify before you propose

One of the most difficult lessons to learn in sales is that not every lead is worth chasing. Mission-driven leaders often fall into the trap of trying to help every potential customer who comes their way, no matter their readiness, fit, or budget. But time and capacity are precious.

So, before you dive into building a proposal, pause and do a quick qualification check of your potential customer by considering questions such as:

- Are we dealing directly with the decision-maker?
- Do they have a budget?
- Do they have a clear need that matches our offering?
- Are they ready to move in the next 3-6 months?

These aren't just questions you should only be asking yourself, either. Don't be afraid to bring up these or other questions you may have with the potential customer directly—so long as you frame them in a way that shows you are trying, above all, to help them, whether or not the conversation ends in you closing a sale. You could present it like this:

> *"Would it be okay if I asked a few questions to make sure this is the right moment—and the right fit—for both of us?"*

Or:

> *"Before we jump into next steps, can I get a quick sense of your timeline and budget? That helps me figure out how we might best be able to support you."*

If the answers to these questions don't paint the rosiest picture, then it's absolutely okay to not proceed at this point. And remember, that doesn't mean you're giving this potential customer a definitive "no"—it's far more of a "let's stay in touch." You can still offer value, share a resource, or check in later, but you don't have to drop everything to chase an opportunity that doesn't look like it will pay off—for either side.

Step 4: Lead with listening on your discovery calls

Your discovery call is the heart of your sales process. It's not a pitch, it's a conversation. It's where trust is either built, or broken.

So, how do you go about building trust on the call?

- **Show up curious.** You're not here to sell—you're here to learn what's really going on.

- **Listen well.** Don't just wait for your turn to speak: let silence do some work, and reflect back what you hear.

- **Ground the conversation in their goals, not your offering.** Let them set the agenda with what matters most to them right now.

- **Share your purpose up front.** Be transparent. Let them know you're here to learn, not pitch—and also to see if there's a real fit between your offering and their needs.

- **Offer insight only when it adds value.** Wait until you've listened before suggesting anything—and tie your ideas directly to what they shared.

- **Stay human.** If something resonates, say so; if you don't know an answer, admit it. Warmth matters.

And, of course, the best way to accomplish all of the above is by asking questions. Find out where they're coming from, where they want to go, and what's currently stopping them from getting there. Ask them:

"What's the biggest challenge you're navigating right now?"

"How are you seeing that show up day to day?"

"What have you tried before?"

"If this goes well, what would be different six months from now?"

Let them talk. Take notes. Reflect back what you hear. And then, after you've done this listening work, you make your suggestion—and when you do, make it personal. Draw on your actual experiences with your previous customers to illustrate how your offering could work for them:

> *"That reminds me of a district we worked with last year—similar context. We focused on building capacity for paraprofessionals, and within two semesters, they saw a 40% increase in certified hires. Would it be helpful if I shared what we did?"*

> *"It sounds like coaching is a priority, but time is tight. We've supported other districts by integrating coaching into existing* PD *sessions—would that be of interest?"*

> *"You mentioned summer being a crunch time. One idea is to pilot with a short summer cohort, and use that data to inform a larger rollout."*

Remember, one real story beats ten PowerPoint slides every time. When you relate to your potential customers in this way, you're not trying to sell them something—you're trying to understand where they are, and whether your work can help. And they'll feel that.

Step 5: Present a thoughtful offer

Your offer is *not* your pitch—it's a direct, honest statement of how you could be the right-fit partner for them. It tells them: "We heard you. We see you. Here's how we can help."

That means starting with a short recap of what they shared with you. Then, walk them through what you're proposing, the outcomes they can expect, and how it will work. Be clear about pricing, timelines, and what's included—no jargon, no fine print.

And when you get to the price? Say it confidently and clearly, in a way that shows respect for their time and their role:

"This package is $18,000 for the semester, and includes weekly coaching sessions, a certification workshop, and implementation support for up to five schools."

"We've structured this as a 12-week pilot for $7,500. It's designed to help you gather real data before deciding on a full-year rollout."

"Our model is $2,000 per site, per semester. That includes digital access, materials, and training for up to ten educators."

Remember, when you get to the stage where you're quoting a price, you're not asking for a favor: you're offering something that is of value to them.

ACTION STEP
BUILD YOUR OFFER TEMPLATE

Draft a simple paragraph that explains your standard offering, including:

- What's included
- Outcomes
- Price

Now, say it all out loud. Revise it as needed until it feels confident and clear.

Step 6: Handle objections with curiosity, not fear

It's important to keep in mind that if a customer raises a concern—about budget, timing, competing priorities, how you stack up against comparable vendors, and so forth—that is *not* a rejection. It's a sign they're seriously considering your offering.

So, lean in, don't back off. Thank them for being honest with you, and ask them if they wouldn't mind answering a couple of quick follow-up questions so that you can get a clearer idea of what's giving them pause. So, for instance, for the four very common objections listed above, try asking things like:

- **Budget**—*"Have you explored using Title III or foundation funding for similar work?"*

- **Timing**—*"What would need to happen for this to move forward next quarter?"*

- **Comparing your organization to others**—*"What matters most to you in choosing a partner?"*

- **Competing priorities**—*"Totally understand—there's a lot on everyone's plate right now. Can I ask what else is front and center for your team this year? That'll help me see where this work might fit, or where it might be better to reconnect down the line."*

Even if the answer they give you ends up being "no," you've still planted a seed. Decision-makers remember the truly thoughtful conversations they've engaged in, and they often end up circling back to those they had them with.

Step 7: Know when (and how) to close
This is the moment when many mission-driven folks freeze. They've had a great call; the partner is nodding along; but then, they stop short of asking for the commitment.

Remember, clarity is not pressure, it's service. You're not being pushy by inviting next steps, you're making it easier for someone to act on something they already care about. If they've stayed on the call, asked good questions, and shared their challenges, they're likely hoping that you'll help guide the way forward.

So that means that you don't have to close with bravado, you just have to close with care. And as always, keep it simple, honest, and direct:

> *"Would you like to move forward with this?"*

> *"Can I send over a draft agreement?"*

> *"Would a mid-January kickoff work for your team?"*

And if they're still not sure if they want to move forward right now? Not a problem:

> *"Totally get it. When would be a good time to check back in?"*

> *"That makes sense. Would it be helpful if I circled back in a few months once things have settled on your end?"*

> *"No rush at all. Is there someone else on your team I should loop in or stay connected with in the meantime?"*

> *"Appreciate your honesty—would it be okay if I sent over a short summary, just so you have it if or when the timing feels better?"*

> *"Totally fair. Can I check back in after your budget planning cycle to see if this might be a better fit then?"*

And then, of course, you follow through on that pledge to reconnect. That's how trust is built and sustained.

Step 8: Keep track of your pipeline

It's inevitable that not all of your proposals are going to land right away, which is why reconnecting is an essential part of the sales long game. But in order to reconnect, you need to keep a clear picture of who you connected with in the first place. You don't want to let potential opportunities get lost in your inbox, your voicemail, or your memory.

This is where your *sales pipeline* comes in. A sales pipeline is simply a record of:

- who you're talking to
- where they are in the sales process
- what the potential value is
- what your next step should be

As always, keep it as simple as the situation requires. Even recording your pipeline on a basic spreadsheet can help you prioritize your time, forecast revenue, and stay organized.

Other tools you can use for this range from a CRM (like Hub-Spot or Airtable) to a simple spreadsheet, like the one below:

ORGANIZATION	CONTACT	STAGE	VALUE	NEXT STEP
Brookdale USD	L. Ramirez	Proposal sent	$18K	Check-in July 1
Metro Charters	D. Singh	Discovery call	$12K	Send proposal May 24
FuturePromise Fdn	E. Sullivan	Inquiry	TBD	Schedule intro call May 30

Remember, if you don't track it, you can't manage it. And if you don't manage it, good opportunities will slip away.

A mission-aligned sales process isn't about becoming someone you're not. It's about creating clarity, building relationships, and making it easy for the right partners to say yes. The more consistent your process becomes, the more confident, and effective, you'll be—and that translates directly to greater sustainability, and greater impact.

But we're not quite done with sales yet. In Step 5, we said that you should discuss pricing with your customers without shame or fear—but it takes a lot of work to get to that point.

Pricing is one of the thorniest, and most emotional, parts of the sales process, especially for education nonprofits.

How do you set prices that reflect your worth, support your mission, and at the same time allow you to remain accessible to your partners? This is what we'll cover in the next stage of the MissionMarket Model.

REFLECTION QUESTIONS

1   How clear is our sales process? Could a new teammate follow it tomorrow?

2   Are we chasing every inquiry, or qualifying leads with intention?

3   Do our discovery calls build trust and insight?

4   How confident are we in naming our price and presenting our offer?

5   What patterns do we see in our pipeline? What's getting stuck, and why?

8

PRICING AND FINANCIAL SUSTAINABILITY
Charging for Impact and Building Staying Power

WHEN SAMIRA launched LearningSpring, a nonprofit dedicated to improving literacy instruction, pricing was the last thing on her mind. She was focused on kids—specifically, the third graders she used to teach who struggled with decoding texts, and the teachers who felt overwhelmed trying to support them.

Samira's team built an exceptional suite of services: literacy coaching, professional development workshops, and a research-informed curriculum supplement. Word spread quickly, and within a year, LearningSpring was flooded with interest from districts across the country.

But something wasn't working. In year two, they had doubled their number of contracts, but ended the year barely breaking even.

Samira realized she had priced their offerings too low. "We were basically paying districts to use our services," she said later, only half-joking. "We nearly grew ourselves out of business."

So the next year, she recalibrated: LearningSpring raised its rates to better reflect the real cost of delivery.

But the response? Crickets. Fewer inbound leads. More proposals that were met with polite declines. The pipeline dried up.

Samira was stuck between two extremes: underpricing and losing money, or overpricing and losing customers. She wasn't margin-driven, but she knew she needed margin to survive.

LIKE SO MANY nonprofit leaders, Samira had realized too late that pricing wasn't just about numbers. Pricing was communication. It was credibility. It was a signal about the value of her work—and a core piece of her organization's long-term sustainability.

For many nonprofit education leaders, pricing is one of the most nerve-racking parts of running a financially sustainable organization. It can stir up a lot of second-guessing, and force us to ask ourselves tough questions like:

"Are we charging too much, or not enough?"

"Will schools be able to afford us?"

"Are we undercutting our own mission by pricing too low?"

"What if we lose the sale because of our quote?"

Those questions aren't just your nerves talking, they're authentic concerns. Pricing is both the ominous cloud hovering at the crucial endpoint of your sales pitch, but also the precondition for being able to sell effectively in the first place. In the last chapter, we covered how to move a sales conversation from interest to commitment—but you can't close a deal confidently if you don't know what to charge. And you can't set pricing that sustains your mission if all you're going off of is guesswork.

The good news is, you don't have to. When pricing is solidly grounded in your overall strategy, it becomes one of your most powerful levers for advancing both your mission and your financial resilience. That's what we're going to learn about in this step of the MissionMarket Model.

In this chapter, we'll discuss how to:

- choose a pricing objective that fits your current stage,

- understand different pricing strategies and when to use them,

- communicate pricing with confidence and clarity, and

- align your pricing with your revenue model, product or service design, and organizational goals.

You don't need to be a finance expert in order to price effectively, but you *do* need a structure. So, let's build one.

How to set prices that are fair, strategic, and mission-aligned

1. Start with your pricing objective

Before you open a spreadsheet or calculate a single cost, take a step back and ask yourself: "What are we trying to accomplish with our pricing right now?"

Because pricing isn't just about breaking even, it's a strategic tool—and like any tool, it works best when you're clear about how you want to use it. A few of the common pricing objectives in the education nonprofit space are:

- **Growing market share**—perhaps you're trying to get your program into more schools, even if that means tighter margins at first. This might be the right move if you're launching a new product or program, or trying to break into a region for the first time.

- **Maximizing net revenue**—if your work is further along, you might be poised to start generating surplus to reinvest in your team, fund R&D, or build a rainy-day reserve. This becomes critical as you start to scale.

- **Signaling value**—in a crowded market, pricing too low can actually backfire on you by making your offering seem less credible or less impactful. A higher price point is an implicit message to potential customers that you're bringing something different to the table.

- **Staying afloat**—the reality is, sometimes you're just trying to survive to fight another day. Cash flow is tight, and you need to bring in revenue fast. It happens, and it's okay. Just make sure it's a short-term move, *not* your default strategy.

Whatever your objective is, make sure you're clear about it to yourself, because your pricing decisions will flow from there.

2. Choose the right pricing strategy

Once you know what you're aiming for, the question then becomes: "How do we figure out what to charge?"

There's no single formula for this, but there are three tried-and-true approaches that can help you: *cost-plus pricing, value-based pricing,* and *competitive pricing.* Most effective pricing strategies blend elements of all three.

Figure 8.1: Comparing Pricing Strategies

STRATEGY	WHAT IT IS	WHEN TO USE IT
Cost-Plus	Add margin to real delivery costs	Baseline for sustainability
Value-Based	High-impact, trust-based relationships	High-impact, trust-based relationships
Competitive	Crowded spaces or emerging product categories	Crowded spaces or emerging product categories

i) Cost-plus pricing

This is your baseline. You add up your costs and tack on a margin. It's not flashy, but it's essential.

You'll want to account for:

- *direct costs* like staff time, materials, travel, etc.

- *indirect costs* like admin support, tech platforms, office space, etc.

- a *reasonable margin* (e.g., 10 to 30%) to cover risk and allow for reinvestment

Just don't forget to include time for onboarding, project management, and follow-up—those hours add up fast.

Think of this strategy as your *floor*. It tells you the lowest you can go while still staying afloat.

ii) Value-based pricing

This approach is more art than science, but it's incredibly powerful. Instead of pricing based on what your product or service costs you, you price it based on what it's *worth* to your customer.

For example:

- If your coaching program reduces teacher turnover in high-need schools, what is that worth to a district spending $75,000+ per lost teacher?

- If your PD helps boost third-grade literacy rates, what are the downstream benefits in terms of student success and accountability ratings?

- If your assessment tool helps a district identify at-risk students earlier, what is that worth in terms of reducing costly interventions later—or even improving graduation rates?

So, how do you arrive at a price that reflects what your product or service's value would be relative to your customers' needs? You can try things like:

- **Talking to your customers.** A simple question like, *"What would this be worth to your team?"* can yield surprising insights. Often, customers have a strong sense of what they're willing to pay, especially if they've worked with other vendors before. They may also surface benefits you hadn't considered: time saved, political capital gained, or smoother implementation. These insights can guide both your pricing and your messaging.

- **Quantify the impact when you can.** Put numbers to your outcomes whenever possible. For instance, if your SEL program reduced disciplinary referrals by 25%, what does that save a school in staff time or alternative placements? If your family engagement workshops led to a 10% increase in attendance, how might that impact funding or school ratings? Quantifying results helps justify your price—and helps buyers make the case internally.

- **Position your price in terms of outcomes, not just hours or materials.** Instead of pricing based on how many coaching hours you provide, focus on what those hours achieve. Say, *"This package supports improved math outcomes for multilingual learners in Grades 3–5,"* rather than, *"This package includes ten hours of PD and two site visits."* Customers aren't buying your time—they're buying the transformation your time enables.

Remember, perceived value isn't just about results: it's also about *trust* (do they believe you'll deliver?), *credibility* (do you have a track record of success?), and *relevance* (does your work speak to their specific challenges right now?). A district leader might pay more for a partner they know can hit the ground running, work within their systems, and help them shine in front of the board. Pricing for value means understanding not just the outcomes—but the broader context in which those outcomes matter.

iii) Competitive pricing

This strategy is all about context. It's not about copying your peers, but about understanding where you sit in the landscape. Paying attention to competitors helps you spot both risks and opportunities. It also helps you understand what your buyers are comparing *you* to, so you can highlight what makes you meaningfully different, not just cheaper or flashier.

Take a look at what similar organizations charge. Look at published pricing, RFP responses, or intel from your network. You might find that everyone is clustered around the same mid-range price point—leaving space to either differentiate with a higher-touch premium offer, or disrupt the market with a more accessible, scaled-down version.

Then, ask yourself:

"Are we positioning ourselves as a premium solution?"

"A scrappy, cost-effective alternative?"

"Something in between?"

Whatever you do, don't race to the bottom. Undercutting competitors might win you a contract, but it can damage your sustainability and your perceived credibility in the long run.

3. Triangulate your price

Having completed the strategic analyses above, you've now got three valuable data points:

i) your *cost floor*

ii) your customer's *perceived value* of your product or service

iii) the *state of the market landscape* you're competing in

Now it's time to *triangulate* those three points—that is, use all three perspectives in order to arrive at a price point for your offering that is financially viable, compelling to your customer, and appropriate within your market.

Figure 8.2: The Pricing Strategy Triad

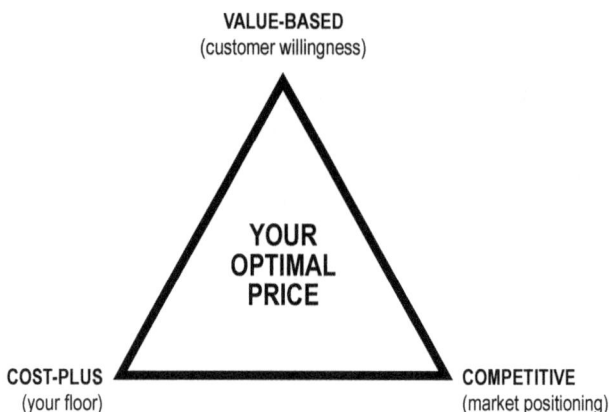

VALUE-BASED
(customer willingness)

**YOUR
OPTIMAL
PRICE**

COST-PLUS
(your floor)

COMPETITIVE
(market positioning)

This step brings your strategy into focus. It helps you land on a number (or a pricing structure) that's not just defensible, but smart. The ideal end result will be a price that covers your costs, reflects your value, and sets you up for sustainability and growth.

Here's how you go about it:

- **Start with your cost-plus minimum.** What's the lowest you can go without losing money? This gives you your *floor*—your guardrail against pricing out of desperation or guilt.

- **Layer in value-based insights.** What are your customers willing to pay for the outcomes you deliver? If your work saves time, boosts results, or solves a top-priority problem, that's definitely worth something—often more than your direct costs would suggest.

- **Scan your competitors in the market.** What are others charging, and how do you compare to them? Even if your work is unique, your buyers are likely evaluating multiple options. Know the range, and be intentional about where you sit within it.

- **Return to your pricing objective.** Are you trying to grow fast? Build reserves? Signal quality? Your pricing isn't just a number, it's a message. Make sure it aligns with your goals and your stage of growth.

Decide on a pricing structure that fits your situation. Common structures include:

- **Tiered pricing** (e.g., basic vs. premium support)

- **Volume discounts** (e.g., lower per-site cost when more schools are involved)

- **Bundled services** (e.g., curriculum + coaching = more value, more margin)

- **Pilot pricing or early-adopter rates** (great for entering a new market or testing a new offering)

Triangulation doesn't guarantee perfection, but it gets you close to the right price for you—the one that sustains your mission and makes sense to your buyers. And remember, the price you arrive at isn't set in stone—it's a living strategy. Revisit it at least once a year, or any time your goals, costs, or market position shift.

4. Communicate your price with confidence

This is the part where many nonprofit leaders start to sweat. You've done the math; you've set the strategy. But now you have to *say the number out loud.*

Here's the secret: clarity is *not* pressure, and confidence is *not* arrogance—it's *alignment.*

So, to begin with:

- **Don't apologize.** Your price sends a message, whether you like it or not. A low price might imply your offering is untested, hard to scale, or not something "serious" districts invest in. A higher price says that this work *matters*—it requires commitment, and is designed for real change. Be intentional about the story your pricing tells, and *own* it.

- **Tie your price to your outcomes.** Instead of leading with deliverables, lead with *impact.* So rather than saying, *"It's $25,000 for twelve coaching sessions,"* say, *"This $25,000 investment has helped districts like yours reduce teacher turnover by 30% and raise ELA scores by twelve points within a year."* Now the price doesn't just sound reasonable—it sounds smart.

- **Use anchors.** Your *anchor* is a reference point that helps your customer interpret the value of your price; in other words, it gives them something to compare it to. For example, you can try citing:

  a) **the cost of the problem**—*"Districts spend over $100,000 a year managing literacy interventions; this coaching and toolkit package comes in at less than a third of that."*

  b) **alternatives in the market**—*"Other providers offer similar support at $40,000 per district. Our model is $28,000, and includes ongoing implementation coaching."*

c) **your own track record**—*"Last year, a similar partnership with Madison Public Schools yielded a 12-point jump in third-grade reading scores—at the same price point we're offering you."*

Anchors create context, and context builds confidence: it helps decision-makers justify the investment to themselves, their team, or their board. Without an anchor, a $25,000 price point can feel arbitrary. With one, it feels reasonable— or even like a smart deal.

- **Build in flexibility (strategically).** You don't have to offer the same price to every partner, but you *do* need a pricing structure that makes sense for your business model, your values, and your goals. Offering a discount every time someone hesitates, or cutting your price just to win a deal, is purely *reactive* flexibility—it's born of desperation, and without any clarity on what you're giving up or how you'll make up the difference.

  Strategic flexibility means offering variation where it's *purposeful*, not purely reactive. It aligns your pricing with your objectives—whether that's growth, access, learning, or positioning. And it ensures that even when your prices vary, your logic doesn't.

  So, if you encounter some hesitation in a potential customer, depending on their situation you could:

  a) suggest *early-adopter discounts* to pilot your offering with a new district segment, because their feedback is valuable and could unlock future sales

  b) offer *volume-based pricing* to multi-site districts, which would give them an incentive to scale the work across multiple schools at once while your margins remain intact

c) propose *pilot rates with clear end dates*, allowing a district to try your program at a lower price while setting expectations for full pricing if they continue.

However you vary your pricing, just remember to be *consistent with your own objectives*. Your pricing flexibility always needs to be *strategic*, not *reactive*.

5. Align your pricing with your revenue model

Your pricing doesn't live in isolation—it sits within your broader *revenue model*. As you'll recall from our work in Chapter 5, your revenue model encompasses the ways in which your organization generates income—whether through services, products, government contracts, philanthropy, or some mix of these. In that chapter, we also diagnosed how scalable and predictable your current model is, and began to map out what might come next.

Here's the link with pricing: the way you *set and structure your prices* should reflect the revenue model you're operating within. Otherwise, you're setting yourself up for frustration: undercharging for labor-intensive work, confusing your customers with inconsistent pricing, creating cash flow gaps, or, worse, veering off-mission because the math no longer works.

Let's walk through the three common nonprofit revenue models we covered in Chapter 5, and how smart pricing supports each one. (Spoiler: most organizations end up in the hybrid zone—but more on that in a moment.)

Figure 8.3: Revenue Model – Pricing Alignment Matrix

REVENUE MODEL	HOW TO PRICE	EXAMPLE
Service-Based	Staff time + margin; retainer packages	$15K coaching package with planning and travel
Product-Based	Scalable, license/subscription model	$5K/year curriculum license
Hybrid	Base + add-ons; clear separation of scope	$10K platform + $7.5K coaching add-on

i) Service-based

This is the classic model for education nonprofits and consulting-style organizations. You're selling time, expertise, and labor—coaching, professional development, technical assistance, research, curriculum design, and so on.

When it comes to pricing in this model:

- **Price based on staff time and delivery costs.** Every hour should count—including prep, travel, and follow-up—not just the time spent "on screen" with clients. If it takes forty hours to deliver a project, price for forty, not thirty.

- **Use packages or retainers.** Instead of billing hourly, offer a flat fee for a scope of work over a semester or school year. This provides predictability for both you and the customer.

- **Avoid over-customization.** Custom projects eat up margins fast. Instead, build repeatable offerings with light tailoring. This lets you scale your impact without constantly reinventing the wheel.

Example: *You offer a $15,000 coaching package that includes eight virtual sessions, one in-person school visit, and two hours of planning support—all of it priced to reflect real delivery costs, plus a 20% margin to sustain your team and operations.*

ii) Product-based

Here, you're selling something that doesn't require hands-on delivery each time, such as curriculum materials, an online platform, a diagnostic tool, or a professional learning course.

For this model:

- **Price for scale.** Your goal is to serve more users without increasing delivery costs. This model shines when marginal costs are low and reach is high.

- **Use licensing or subscription models.** Monthly or annual pricing supports predictable revenue and long-term planning, for both you and the customer.

- **Anchor price to outcomes, not features.** Don't just list what's inside the product, focus on what it helps districts achieve (e.g., "ten-point reading gains" or "25% drop in behavioral referrals").

Example: *Your ELA curriculum is licensed at $5,000 per district per year, with optional add-ons like a $2,500 virtual training package or a $1,500 implementation support bundle.*

iii) Hybrid

This is where many education nonprofits actually live— offering both products *and* services. Maybe you've built a great curriculum and also provide coaching, or you have a diagnostic tool as well as technical assistance to help districts use the data well.

The hybrid model is powerful, but it also requires clarity and coordination. Here's how to get it right:

- **Separate core offerings from add-ons.** Be clear about what's included in your base price (e.g., access to the platform) versus what's optional (e.g., coaching, customization). This helps manage customer expectations and prevents scope creep.

- **Bundle strategically.** Think through what combinations will be most useful to your customers. For example, a bundled package of a tool + training + follow-up support might offer more value (and margin) than selling each separately. "What makes sense" here means: does the bundle help the customer implement successfully, and does it align with your delivery capacity?

- **Match your price to the level of support.** The same product can support very different price points depending on how much guidance you provide. A self-serve curriculum might be $3,000; a fully supported implementation package might be $15,000. The lesson? Price reflects not just what you're delivering, but how hands-on you are in making it successful.

Example: *A district buys your assessment platform for $10,000. Then, they add a $7,500 coaching and data analysis package to ensure strong implementation. The total deal is $17,500—higher value for them, higher sustainability for you.*

The bottom line is, when your pricing and revenue model are aligned, everything works better. Your messaging is clearer; you feel more confident in your pricing conversations; your operations run smoother; and your team can deliver what you promised, without burnout.

And remember, none of this needs to (or should) remain static. Your revenue model and your pricing strategy should evolve together as your organization grows. What worked when you had three clients and a Google Doc may not work when you have thirty clients and a delivery team. Adapt intentionally, and your pricing will become one of your strongest tools for sustainability.

Your price isn't just what you charge: it's what you *promise* to your partners, your funders, and your team. When your price reflects your value—and your values—it becomes a tool for advancing your mission, not competing with it. You're not "selling out" by charging for your product or service: you're ensuring you can stay in the fight.

So, say the number out loud. And say it like your work matters—because it does.

REFLECTION QUESTIONS

1   What is your current pricing objective—and is it the right one for your stage of growth?

2   Have you clearly calculated your cost floor, and are you confident it includes all delivery-related expenses?

3   How would your customers describe the value of your offering? Have you ever asked?

4   Where do you sit in the market relative to your peers—and is your pricing telling the right story?

5   Is your pricing aligned with your revenue model, or are there disconnects that might create confusion or strain?

9

SCALING AND OPERATIONALIZING EARNED REVENUE
Turning Strategy into a System

ON ANY GIVEN Tuesday, you could find Lila—the executive director of the scrappy, mission-driven K–12 nonprofit Voices in Schools—trying to do six jobs at once. On this particular morning, she was hunched over her laptop in the corner of a crowded co-working space, toggling between a grant application that was due in four hours, a school district contract she'd been "just about to finish" for three weeks, and an email from her board chair that was gently but persistently asking how things were going on the revenue diversification front.

Lila's organization specialized in helping districts improve instruction and outcomes for multilingual learners (MLLs). Their school-based coaching, dual-language curriculum audits, and community engagement strategies had earned praise from superintendents and local media alike. But, when it came to converting all that goodwill into consistent earned revenue, things kept falling apart.

Lila wasn't new to this. She'd read the books, bookmarked the webinars, and even started a CRM trial. She was in no way opposed to the concept of sales, but she just couldn't figure out how to build a system that didn't require cloning infinite versions of herself. Her team kept asking about follow-ups; a promising lead from Tulsa had gone cold; her Mailchimp campaign had fizzled; and a Google Sheet of "warm leads" hadn't been touched since October.

Meanwhile, she was onboarding new coaches, submitting a funder report, and prepping for a board retreat where she'd have to present (gulp) a "growth strategy."

Lila's vision for Voices in Schools was clear. The impact was real. The market demand was there.

What she didn't have was a *system*.

BEFORE YOU LET that ominously italicized word just above freak you out, let's take a moment to appreciate how far you've come by this point in the MissionMarket Model.

You've laid the groundwork for a strong earned revenue strategy. You've clarified your customer segments; crafted a compelling value proposition; determined an appropriate revenue model; defined your marketing strategy; worked out your sales tactics; and priced your offerings with intention, an awareness of the landscape in which you're operating, and an accurate assessment of the value of what you bring to the table.

Now comes the part that separates hopeful pilots from organizations that can create real, sustainable growth: *scaling* and *operationalizing*.

Scaling means building enough structure to help your organization grow without losing your mind, or your mission.

If you keep relying solely on yourself or a few heroic staff members to keep everything running, growth will only stretch you thinner. What you want is smart, streamlined, *replicable* systems that can help you deliver your work with consistency and care.

Operationalizing means building a sales and delivery engine that doesn't fall apart when you get busy, go on vacation, or shift your attention to a major funder or strategic initiative. It means your systems have your back, even when you're not in the driver's seat. It means your team knows what to do, when to do it, and where to find what they need. It means no more 11 p.m. Slack messages asking, "Do we have a version of this proposal from last time?" or realizing too late that a promising lead never got a follow-up.

When you operationalize, you're not just working harder—you're working smarter. You're creating rhythm, not chaos. And you're giving your mission the structure it needs to grow.

When you operationalize your revenue function, you unlock:

- **Consistency**—you're no longer chasing one-off wins

- **Scalability**—your growth isn't limited by your own calendar

- **Alignment**—sales and delivery work in harmony, not in conflict

- **Freedom**—you finally get your time back to lead

In this chapter, we'll work through how to scale and operationalize your revenue function, step by step. You don't need a giant team or fancy software to make this happen—just clarity, consistency, and a commitment to making your systems work for *you*, not the other way around.

How to build a scalable earned revenue operation

1. Map your revenue operations workflow

Every organization has a workflow, whether it's written down or not. The goal here is to make yours visible and intentional. A basic revenue operations workflow might include:

- **Awareness**—how do new prospects hear about you?

- **Inquiry**—what happens when someone raises their hand?

- **Sales conversation**—who takes the call? Sends the proposal? Follows up?

- **Close**—how do you finalize the agreement and set expectations?

- **Delivery**—who's responsible for actually doing the work?

- **Renewal**—how do you stay in touch and invite them to work with you again?

Write out the steps above and assign names to each one. Even if you're a team of three and the same person shows up in every box, that's okay—the point is clarity. You can't improve what you haven't mapped.

Figure 9.1: Revenue Operations Workflow Map

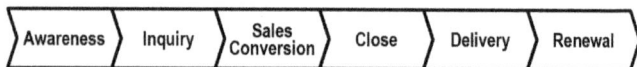

| Awareness | Inquiry | Sales Conversion | Close | Delivery | Renewal |

2. Define who owns what

In a nonprofit's early days, one person—usually the executive director or founder—does everything: marketing, sales, client work, follow-up, and so on. But if you want to grow, you need to start dividing up and defining the work.

Break your earned revenue operation into four core functions:

i) **Marketing**—who's getting your name out there? Who writes the newsletter, posts on LinkedIn, attends events?

ii) **Sales**—who's leading discovery calls, sending proposals, tracking follow-up?

iii) **Customer success**—who onboards clients, checks in, handles renewals?

iv) **Delivery**—who's doing the actual work of coaching, facilitating, designing, etc.?

Create a simple matrix or chart of who owns each area. You might end up seeing your own name in every column, and that's fine—for now. But even writing it down helps you spot opportunities to delegate, outsource, or systematize.

If proposal formatting, CRM upkeep, or sending outreach emails is draining your team's energy, consider outsourcing or automating those admin-heavy pieces. Your time is precious. Protect it.

3. Choose (and actually use) the right tools

As we said above, you don't need a million-dollar tech stack to properly operationalize your organization. But you do need a few core tools, and a shared commitment to using them consistently.

At a minimum, you'll want to have:

- a **CRM** (customer relationship management tool) to track leads, contacts, and deals (e.g., Think HubSpot, Airtable, Copper)

- a **marketing platform** for email outreach and campaigns (e.g., Mailchimp, Substack, ConvertKit)

- a folder of **templates** (proposals, pricing sheets, outreach emails, intake forms, etc.) that is accessible to all the members of your team

- a simple **dashboard** (even just a Google Sheet) to track active deals, projected revenue, and sales status

Remember, a basic system your team actually uses is better than a perfect system no one touches.

4. Build your sales asset library

Here's where many small teams burn time: reinventing proposals, emails, or onboarding docs over and over again. Let's stop that cycle.

Create a centralized folder—your **sales asset library**—with your core materials:

- a mission-aligned **pitch deck**

- a clear, easy-to-understand **pricing sheet**

- **email templates** for initial outreach, follow-up, scheduling, etc.

- **intake forms** and **onboarding checklists**

Save your sales asset library to a shared drive, and update it quarterly. Most importantly, train your team to actually use it. If it lives in someone's head or on a single laptop, it's not a system—it's a bottleneck.

5. Monitor the engine

Now that your sales system is up and running, you need a way to check the gauges.

Hold a short (30-minute) biweekly check-in with your team to review:

- How many active leads are in the pipeline?

- What stage is each opportunity in?

- What's closing, and what's stalling?

- What's your delivery capacity? Are people overbooked, or underutilized?

- Are you getting feedback from current customers?

This meeting doesn't need slides or spreadsheets, it just needs focus. Use what you learn to make smart choices about where to follow up, when to hire, or what to tweak in your messaging.

And *don't keep this info siloed.* Share it with your team. When everyone can see the full picture, you avoid surprises and stay aligned on what's coming next.

6. Plan for delivery at scale

Now let's talk about what happens when success hits.

Say you land three new district contracts in the same month. Exciting, right? But the question is: Are you actually ready to fulfill those commitments?

Growth is great, but unmanaged growth can overwhelm your team and erode your quality. So ask yourself now, before you hit that tipping point:

- How many clients can we serve at once, without sacrificing quality?

- What triggers the need to bring on a new hire or contractor?

- Can our onboarding systems handle a surge?

- Is our delivery model documented well enough for others to replicate it?

To help you determine the answers to these questions, start building SOPs (standard operating procedures) that capture how you deliver your work. Train new facilitators or coaches using these systems. Create repeatable onboarding flows. And most importantly, don't wait until you're in crisis mode to figure it out.

Scaling isn't about doing more—it's about doing what works, again and again, without reinventing the wheel.

THREE SIGNS YOU NEED BETTER SYSTEMS

1   You're the bottleneck: If sales or delivery stalls every time you're away, it's time to document and delegate.

2   Things fall through the cracks: Lost leads, overdue follow-ups, forgotten renewals are red flags of inadequate systems.

3   You dread growth: If the thought of scaling up creates anxiety rather than excitement, your infrastructure needs attention.

Operationalizing your organization doesn't mean becoming a bureaucracy. It means building a *rhythm*—a flywheel that turns more easily with each rotation.

Some organizations find themselves scaling before they've fully operationalized, responding to momentum, demand, or funding. Others deliberately operationalize first, building the foundation they'll need to grow with confidence. There's no one right order: what matters is that both become part of your sustainability journey.

When it's done right, operationalization allows you to free yourself from reactive chaos. You gain clarity, control, and confidence. You stop sprinting for every contract, and start scaling the impact you were built for.

REFLECTION QUESTIONS

1   What parts of your revenue process feel messy or overly dependent on you?

2   If you doubled your contracts next month, what would break?

3   What steps can you take this quarter to make your revenue operations more repeatable?

4   How can you build a sales and delivery system that reflects your organization's values?

10

MIXED FUNDING MODELS
Where Earned Revenue Fits in Your Bigger Financial Picture

IT WAS 9:07 A.M. on a Thursday when Simone's phone buzzed.

"Hi Simone, it's Kavita from the Oakdale Foundation," said the voice on the other end. "Got a few minutes later this week to talk? We're exploring some innovation grants, and your name keeps coming up."

Simone, the executive director of LitReach, had worked with Oakdale before: small grants for community engagement, a few joint events with grantees. But this sounded different.

"I'll send a time," Kavita continued. "By the way, love what you're doing on the earned revenue side. Honestly, it gives us more confidence that this thing is built to last."

After the call ended, Simone just sat there for a moment. That last comment echoed in her mind.

"More confidence?" Because of earned revenue? That wasn't what she'd expected to hear when she first launched LitReach.

In the early days, Simone, like many nonprofit leaders, had worried that charging for her services might make funders question her commitment to equity; she feared it would look like "going commercial." But over the past two

years, she and her team had built out a professional learning offering for school districts grounded in their literacy
equity work. It started small—just a handful of contracts—
but momentum had grown. Now, earned revenue made up
about 30% of their annual budget.

And the very positive irony of this situation was that their
very success was now helping unlock *more* philanthropic
capital, not less.

Simone thought back to the long hours of pricing strategy, sales calls, and building delivery systems—efforts that
had once felt like detours from "real" impact work. But now,
those systems were being seen for what they really were: a
foundation for scale. A way to turn grant-funded pilots into
enduring solutions.

And the funders weren't walking away. They were leaning in.

BY THIS STAGE of the MissionMarket Model, you've clarified your audience, shaped your value proposition, designed
a revenue model, set prices, and started building a sales and
marketing engine. Now you're not just doing good work—
you're getting paid for it in ways that sustain your mission.

But, despite its importance, earned revenue is rarely the
full picture for education nonprofits. Most of these organizations operate with multiple funding streams—and for
good reason. A healthy funding model blends revenue from
different sources, each of which plays a distinct role in pow-
ering your impact.

In this chapter, we'll zoom out so we can see how earned
revenue fits within your broader financial architecture. We'll
explore how a mixed funding model can:

- provide stability across fiscal years,

- unlock philanthropic support for scale,

- position your organization as both credible and ambitious, and

- help you build a long-term vision that funders, partners, and team members can rally around.

Whether you're trying to get out of the cycle of grant-to-grant survival, or are seeking a more intentional way to grow, this chapter is your invitation to think bigger. You've done the work to start building revenue. Now it's time to layer in the strategy that can help you go further—with confidence, clarity, and staying power.

The power of a mixed model

What exactly do we mean by a "mixed funding model"? At its simplest, it's a combination of different revenue streams—earned income, philanthropic grants, government contracts, corporate sponsorships, and so forth—that together support the financial health and strategic goals of your organization.

For many education nonprofits, this kind of blended approach isn't just helpful, it's essential. Earned revenue can provide autonomy and sustainability, but it often takes time to grow and can fluctuate based on seasons, school budgets, or shifting demand. Philanthropy can be catalytic and expansive, but it's also competitive, often restricted, and rarely guaranteed year to year. Government funding, meanwhile, can be large and durable, but slow, bureaucratic, and complex to manage.

Each source comes with its own benefits and limitations. The trick lies in understanding the distinct role each can play, and in designing a funding mix that makes them work together. When done well, a mixed model gives you more stability, more strategic options, and more room to focus on your mission without constantly worrying about where the next check will come from.

Figure 10.1: The Power of a Mixed Model – Funding Source Comparison Table

FUNDING SOURCE	STRENGTHS	CHALLENGES
Earned Revenue	Flexible, signals traction	Grows slowly, seasonal cycles
Philanthropy	Catalytic, funds R&D	Competitive, often restricted
Government Contracts	Large, durable	Bureaucratic, complex to manage
Corporate Partnerships	Brand-building, flexible	Often small or one-time support

Later in this chapter, we'll walk through how to model your own revenue mix—looking not just at where the money is coming from, but what each stream is meant to do. For now, let's take a closer look at the two pillars that often form the foundation of a healthy funding model: earned revenue, and philanthropy.

Earned revenue—Your engine for flexibility and control

When schools or districts pay for your services, that income usually comes with fewer restrictions than a grant. That's important. Earned revenue can help you:

- cover core operations (staff time, tech tools, admin support, etc.)

- smooth out cash flow between grant cycles

- demonstrate value and traction to external stakeholders

- create a feedback loop between delivery and financial health

The downside is that earned revenue often grows gradually; it can fluctuate, and, in the K–12 education sector especially, sales cycles are long and seasonal. So while earned revenue is powerful, it can't always stand alone, especially in your early years.

Philanthropy—Your catalyst for innovation and access

Philanthropic grants aren't just about filling budget gaps. Used strategically, they can:

- underwrite the development of new offerings
- subsidize access for schools that can't afford full-price services
- fund impact measurement and field building
- signal credibility to other funders and partners

When you pair philanthropy with earned revenue, something powerful happens. You can use grant dollars to build or expand offerings, and then use earned revenue to sustain them. You shift from dependency to durability.

ACTION STEP
PLAN THE PHILANTHROPY

What's one area where grant funding could unlock future earned revenue? (e.g., content development, pilot programs, measurement capacity)

Write it down. That's your next funder pitch.

The "Sweet Spot"—Strategic sequencing and role clarity

The goal of exploring multiple funding sources is not to replace one revenue stream with another. It's to clarify what each stream is for, and how they work together.

For example:

- **Philanthropy** funds R&D, allowing you to build a new curriculum or pilot a coaching model

- **Earned revenue** sustains the model, once it has been tested and validated

- A **government contract** expands the reach of the model, allowing you to serve more schools and districts

- **Corporate partnerships** fund storytelling or outreach, helping your work build momentum

Each of these funding sources does something different, but when you line them up with intention, they become more than the sum of their parts. That's the beauty of a mixed funding model: it creates balance. Where one stream is flexible, another is stable. Where one helps you innovate, another helps you scale. The result is an organization that's more resilient, more nimble, and better equipped to deliver consistent impact, even when conditions shift.

And here's why that matters to funders: they want to invest in organizations that are built to last. When you can show that you're not relying on a single funding source to carry the full weight of your mission, it signals maturity. It tells them you've thought ahead; that you're managing risk; and that you understand your business model, as well as your program model. Funders don't expect you to be self-sufficient, but they do want to know that their dollars are helping build something durable, not just propping it up.

So when you can tell this story with confidence—when you can point to a model where each dollar has a purpose and a pathway—you give everyone more reason to believe in your growth. Funders lean in. Districts take you seriously. And your team sees a future they can build toward.

Figure 10.2: Strategic Sequencing – How Funding Sources Evolve Over Time

STAGE	FUNDING TYPE		ROLE
Early Stage	Philanthropy	>	Pilot/Build Infrastructure
Growth Stage	Earned Revenue	>	Sustain Delivery + Prove Traction
Scaling Stage	Government + Corporate	>	Expand Reach + Broaden Influence

ACTION STEP
FIND THE SWEET SPOT

Complete this sentence:

"*Our earned revenue gives us* _____, *while our grant funding allows us to* _____."

If your answers feel vague or lopsided, it's time to rebalance.

What funders really think about earned revenue

Many nonprofit leaders worry that focusing on earned revenue might alienate funders. But here's what we've heard from dozens of education grantmakers: *earned revenue is a signal of strength.*

When you demonstrate:

- a clear product-market fit,
- a functioning sales and delivery system,
- smart pricing and business-model thinking, and
- discipline in tracking outcomes and revenue,

it shows that you're building for the long haul.

In fact, some funders will explicitly ask how you plan to sustain your work beyond their grant. Others will only fund pilots that have a path to earned revenue or broader adoption. And increasingly, funders want to know how their dollars can be used to *unlock* other sources of support, rather than their contribution having to carry the whole load.

To that point, many funders are actually willing to *fund* the build-out of your earned revenue strategy. They know that market-based models don't just "happen": they require infrastructure. That might mean helping you invest in a CRM, hire a director of partnerships, or develop a content marketing strategy—all in service of your long-term sustainability.

Modeling your revenue mix

By this point, you've built out several crucial components of your Sustainability Plan—namely:

- who you serve
- what value you deliver
- how you reach them
- how you price your offerings
- how you close deals
- how you operationalize delivery

Modeling your revenue mix is the final piece of that puzzle. It's where strategy meets numbers, and where vision becomes viability. It gives you, your board, and your funders a shared understanding of your path to sustainability, and helps you lead with intention, not just intuition.

That means:

- projecting what percentage of your revenue will come from earned income

- identifying which philanthropic dollars are renewable vs. one-time

- clarifying what each revenue stream will support (e.g., core ops, innovation, expansion)

- creating a plan for how you'll grow or rebalance your funding model over time

Let's return to Simone's story at the beginning of this chapter to see how she was able to adjust LitReach's revenue mix over the course of the organization's evolution.

Two years before that unexpected phone call from Kavita at the Oakdale Foundation, Simone was in a very different place.

At the time, LitReach was almost entirely reliant on philanthropic grants: 100% of its funding came from foundations. While those grants had helped launch their literacy equity work and attract early recognition, the funding was uneven and unpredictable. Some years brought in more money than they knew how to spend; in other years, Simone found herself staring at payroll projections with a pit in her stomach.

It was a classic feast-or-famine cycle, and it made everything harder. Simone couldn't plan for growth; she couldn't invest in infrastructure; and she was constantly shifting her team's attention between fundraising, reporting, and last-minute pivots when funding fell through. It wasn't just stressful, it was unsustainable.

That's when she decided to build a more intentional, mixed-source funding strategy. With help from her board treasurer and a trusted advisor, Simone began modeling different scenarios for what a healthier funding mix could look like. They projected that earned income could grow to 30% within three years, especially if they refined their professional learning offerings and improved district renewal rates. They also took a hard look at their philanthropic grants, identifying which ones were likely to be renewed and which were time-bound or one-off.

Figure 10.3: Simone's Funding Matrix – Before and After

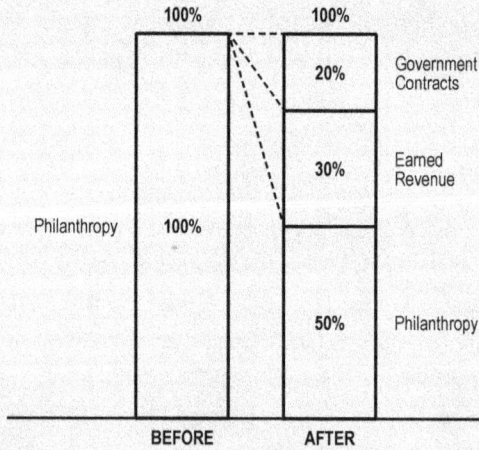

Next, they clarified the role each funding source would play. District contracts would cover core operations—staff time, materials, delivery. Philanthropic dollars would be used more strategically: to fund new content development, pilot innovative models, and subsidize access for under-resourced schools. Simone also launched a plan to pursue multi-year government contracts to support expansion into rural districts, where need was high but earned revenue potential was lower.

Then came the rebalancing plan. Simone set a goal to shift at least 50% of their fixed operating costs onto earned revenue over time. That would free up grant dollars for innovation, not administration. She also began cultivating one new anchor funder—someone who wouldn't just write a check for programs, but who would invest in LitReach's infrastructure: a Director of Partnerships, a new CRM, and dedicated time for the leadership team to focus on sustainability.

Two years later, when Kavita from Oakdale called, the shift was already underway. LitReach's revenue model still included philanthropy, but it wasn't dependent on it. Simone had a clear story to tell: a roadmap for growth, a plan for sustainability, and a funding model that made the work stronger, not shakier.

She wasn't chasing opportunities anymore. She was choosing them.

When Simone launched LitReach, she grappled with a common tension: could she grow sustainably while staying deeply mission-aligned? As her journey revealed—and as you've explored throughout this chapter—a mixed funding model isn't a compromise, it's a strategic strength. By blending earned revenue with philanthropic support, government contracts, and thoughtful partnerships, you position your organization to thrive amid the complexities of the K-12 landscape.

Earned revenue provides flexibility and autonomy, giving you room to invest directly in your mission. Philanthropy and strategic partnerships can accelerate your innovation, support equitable access, and provide the resources needed for bold, catalytic moves. Together, these funding streams form a financial ecosystem that fuels your work not just for a grant cycle, but for the long haul.

Funders and district leaders alike are drawn to organizations that approach financial sustainability thoughtfully. Like Simone experienced, your intentional approach to blending revenue streams signals confidence, credibility, and staying power. It demonstrates that you're not here to just pilot great ideas, but to sustain and scale meaningful solutions over time.

By embracing a mixed funding model, you build the foundation your organization needs to confidently pursue ambitious goals, amplify your impact, and serve students and communities effectively, year after year.

REFLECTION QUESTIONS

1   How do your current funding streams work together, or compete with each other?

2   What role do you want earned revenue to play in your organization's future?

3   How might you reframe your philanthropic conversations to highlight your sustainability strategy?

4   If a funder called tomorrow and asked, "How are you thinking about growth?" what would you say?

CONCLUSION
Building Something
That Lasts

WHEN YOU FIRST picked up this book, you might have been hopeful, but maybe a little skeptical. The idea of building a revenue engine probably felt both urgent and intimidating. You may have been asking yourself questions like:

"Can we really generate earned revenue without compromising our equity-centered mission?"

"How do we 'sell' without feeling like we're selling out?"

"Will foundations think we need them less if we start charging for our services?"

"What if we just don't know where to start?"

But now, here you are. You've covered the theory, tactics, and mindset of building an earned revenue engine for your organization. You've thought deeply about how to serve your students, families, and educators more sustainably. You've learned how to identify your customers, shape your offerings, articulate your value, and structure pricing that supports—not undermines—your impact. You've begun to see that financial sustainability and social mission are not opposing forces—in fact, they can reinforce each other.

And, most importantly, you've come to realize that you're not just running a program—you're leading a movement.

Your Sustainability Plan: A review

In education, we talk a lot about closing achievement gaps, expanding opportunity, and reimagining systems. Your organization likely exists to do one or more of those things. But here's the truth we don't talk about enough: programs that can't sustain themselves don't scale. And programs that don't scale can't create the system-level impact our kids deserve.

That's why this work matters. What you're building isn't just a service, a toolkit, or a pilot program. You're building *capacity*—within your organization, your team, and your community. You're building staying power for ideas that can move the field.

You've laid the groundwork for that by creating a *Sustainability Plan* that connects your mission to the market in which it has to operate. You've developed:

A mission-rooted theory of change
- You know what long-term impact you're trying to achieve.

- You understand the causal pathway from activities to outcomes.

- You've clarified your assumptions and aligned your work accordingly.

A clear understanding of your customers
- You've identified who *benefits from*, who *uses*, who *influences*, and who buys your product, service, or program.

- You've then focused your sales efforts on the buyers—the *right-fit customers* who are both aligned with the impact you're trying to create, and have the authority and the budget to support your work financially.

- You've constructed *customer personas* to better understand your right-fit customers' pain points, priorities, and goals.

A compelling value proposition

- You've defined what makes your offering uniquely valuable.

- You've articulated how it solves a specific problem, in a way that will resonate with district decision-makers, funders, and partners.

- You've grounded your messaging in real-world outcomes.

A smart revenue model

- You've selected the model(s) that best fit your offering and your goals.

- You've considered scalability, seasonality, adaptability, and capacity.

- You've made room for both earned revenue and philanthropic contributions.

A mission-aligned marketing and sales strategy

- You've built awareness, trust, and credibility. Your customers know who you are, and what you have to offer them.

- You've implemented a respectful, repeatable, and mission-aligned sales process founded in collaboration, not coercion.

- You've managed your pipeline and moved opportunities forward.

A pricing strategy that supports impact
- You've set prices that reflect your worth and support sustainability, while also aligning with market norms.
- You've built in flexibility without undermining consistency.
- You've learned how to talk about price with confidence and clarity.

An operational plan that can scale
- You've built templates, systems, and team roles to support growth.
- You've connected revenue to delivery capacity and staff utilization.
- You've created visibility into your pipeline and performance.

A mixed funding model that builds resilience
- You've positioned earned revenue as part of an overall funding strategy that invites both philanthropy and public investment.
- You've used earned revenue to unlock greater leverage and confidence with funders.

Each piece of the plan builds on the last. Each chapter you've read has been a building block—part of a larger blueprint for financial and strategic resilience. You've started to shift from surviving on grants, to thriving on purpose.

What you're facing: Navigating the K–12 landscape

The K-12 education system has its own rhythm, constraints, and politics. Selling into school systems is not like selling software to a business. Decision-makers aren't spending their own money; they're often balancing:

- complex state and federal funding streams
- budget cycles tied to the school year
- staffing shortages and high burnout
- ever-shifting policy mandates
- community and board politics
- deep equity challenges

District leaders may love what you offer, but still take six months to buy it, or need board approval, or be waiting for Title I funds to be released. All of that can make the earned revenue path feel messy, slow, and frustrating.

But it also means that when you *do* earn a school system's trust, it can lead to multi-year partnerships, deep systems change, and scaled impact. By understanding the unique contours of this system, and building revenue strategies that work with—not against—the grain, you become a more effective leader: one who speaks both mission and market, and who's not just pitching products but solving real problems.

Where you go from here

Picture this:

- You sit down with a district leader and *know* how to walk them through your offer—with pricing, outcomes, and next steps ready.

- A funder invites you to apply for a grant and says, "Your earned revenue model made us confident you could scale this work."

- You launch a new initiative without scrambling for startup funding, because your core services already support the infrastructure.

- You take a *real* vacation, and the work continues without you.

- Your board retreats are about growth strategy, not emergency fundraising.

- Your team feels confident about the future, because the foundation is strong.

These are not hypotheticals. In our work with EdSolutions, we've seen them happen for real organizations, all the time. And all of these outcomes are well within your reach.

Now it's your turn.

Some of you reading this book may have already begun to use its tools and resources to start drafting your Sustainability Plan. If so, great—keep looking to it as your North Star. Revisit it quarterly. Share it with your team. Refine it as you learn more.

But even if you haven't yet started implementing the lessons in this book, you've already accomplished the crucial transformation you need to make your work sustainable: you've changed the way you *think* about how your mission relates to the market. You've asked yourself hard questions. You've interrogated your assumptions. And you've begun to understand the true value you can bring to the people who need what you have to offer.

So, when it comes to building your Sustainability Plan, just start where you are. Block out a few hours to work on it. Pick one section to focus on at a time. You don't need to do everything at once—you just need to keep going.

And if you're feeling unsure or overwhelmed, that's normal. It just means you're doing real work. Work that will outlast a funding cycle. Work that can transform what's possible for the students and communities you serve.

So, as you start getting down to that work, take a moment to pause and celebrate. You've already taken a step that many nonprofit leaders never take. And in that, you've started building a model that's designed to last.

Let's say it all one more time, clearly:

- Earned revenue is not a distraction from your mission—it's a way to sustain it.

- Sales is not manipulation—it's connection.

- Marketing is not fluff—it's storytelling in the service of impact.

- Pricing is not greed—it's a reflection of your value and your vision.

This journey isn't about becoming more like a business: it's about building a future where equity-focused, student-centered, mission-driven work isn't an unrealizable dream, but a sustainable force in the education system.

And you? You're the kind of leader who can make that future real.

Keep building. Keep leading. Keep going.

We're cheering you on.

APPENDIX
CivicRoots Sustainability Plan (Exemplar)

At the very beginning of this book, we met Alicia, the executive director of CivicRoots. She was a passionate leader whose organization was making a meaningful impact through civics education, but was struggling to achieve sustainable growth.

Throughout this book, you've worked through each step of the MissionMarket Model to learn how to build a clear, mission-aligned approach to earned revenue and organizational sustainability. What follows is the full Sustainability Plan for CivicRoots, written in Alicia's voice. It's a fictional—but realistic—example of what it looks like when all the pieces of this book come together. I've included this example to give you a clear, concrete reference point as you begin drafting your own plan.

Use this as a model, not a mold. Your organization is unique, and your Sustainability Plan will reflect your mission, context, and goals. But if you've worked through the chapters, Action Steps and Reflection Questions in this book, you already have everything you need to begin writing your own.

Let this plan serve as a guide, and a reminder that, with strategy, clarity, and heart, sustainability is possible.

Introduction

CivicRoots is dedicated to transforming civics education in schools serving historically underserved communities. Our goal is to empower educators and engage students, developing the next generation of informed, active citizens.

This Sustainability Plan outlines our strategic approach to scaling our impact through earned revenue and philanthropic partnerships. It provides clarity on our mission, how we measure impact, and our strategy for financial sustainability and growth.

Part 1: Theory of change

1.1 Defining the problem

The crisis in civic education

Civics proficiency among U.S. students is alarmingly low. The most recent National Assessment of Educational Progress (NAEP) found that only 24% of eighth-grade students performed at or above proficiency levels in civics. This deficit is even more pronounced among students in under-resourced schools, widening gaps in civic participation and undermining the foundations of democracy.

Research indicates that inadequate civic education leads to lower rates of civic engagement, voting participation, and community involvement, disproportionately affecting historically marginalized communities. Schools serving predominantly low-income, Black, Latino, and immigrant student populations frequently lack access to high-quality, culturally responsive civics education resources.

Opportunity for impact

High-quality civics education has proven benefits. Students who engage deeply in civics education demonstrate higher rates of civic participation, voting, and leadership later in life. For instance, a study by Tufts University showed that students exposed to rigorous civic learning programs are 40% more likely to engage in community service and 20% more likely to vote in adulthood.

Pilot implementations of CivicRoots' curriculum have demonstrated significant promise. Teachers consistently report increased student engagement, improved critical thinking skills, and enhanced classroom discussions about civic responsibility and community participation. In one pilot district, student civic proficiency scores increased by an average of 18% within a single academic year.

1.2 CivicRoots' mission and vision

Mission
CivicRoots equips teachers and schools with rigorous, culturally responsive civics curricula and professional development to empower students—especially those from historically underserved communities—to become active, informed participants in our democracy.

Vision
Every student, regardless of background, receives meaningful civics education that prepares them to participate actively and equitably in civic life and democratic processes.

1.3 Our theory of change

Long-term outcome
Our ultimate aim is to significantly increase civic knowledge, skills, and engagement among students in underserved districts, closing the civic participation gap that undermines democracy.

Intermediate outcomes

- Teachers consistently use CivicRoots curricula and instructional strategies effectively in their classrooms.

- Students demonstrate measurable growth in civic knowledge, critical thinking skills, and community engagement.

- Districts institutionalize civics education as a fundamental component of their educational framework, expanding access to high-quality civics learning.

Core activities and strategies

- **Curriculum development:** We provide evidence-based, culturally responsive curriculum resources specifically designed to engage students from diverse backgrounds.

- **Professional development:** We deliver targeted training and coaching to educators, enhancing their capacity to facilitate effective civics instruction.

- **Strategic district partnerships:** We work closely with district leaders to integrate CivicRoots curricula and professional development across schools systematically.

Stakeholders and beneficiaries

- **Direct beneficiaries:** Students in historically underserved communities, particularly Black, Latino, immigrant, and low-income youth.

- **Primary stakeholders:** *Teachers* and *instructional leaders* implementing the curricula; *district administrators* responsible for curricular decisions; *policymakers* interested in equitable civic outcomes.

Underlying assumptions

- Districts recognize civics education as vital but require accessible, compelling evidence of impact and practical resources.

- Effective civics instruction depends on well-supported educators who have both resources and ongoing professional learning opportunities.

Part 2: Sustainability Plan

The following sections outline CivicRoots' strategic approach to achieving long-term financial sustainability and scaling our mission-driven impact.

2.1 Identifying target customers

CivicRoots primarily targets medium-to-large urban and suburban public school districts with significant populations of underserved students. Our key *customer persona* is district Chief Academic Officers (CAOs), who seek evidence-based civics curricula and measurable outcomes to improve equity and civic engagement.

2.2 Value proposition and positioning

Our unique value proposition is the delivery of culturally responsive civics curricula coupled with comprehensive professional development. We differentiate ourselves through proven results, validated by increased student proficiency scores and engagement metrics in pilot districts.

2.3 Revenue model

Our primary revenue model consists of service-based contracts with school districts. We offer the CivicRoots Comprehensive Partnership, which includes full curriculum access, professional learning, implementation support, and annual impact assessment reports. Typical contracts range from $75,000 to $150,000 per district annually, depending on district size and services provided.

2.4 Marketing and outreach strategy

We leverage *content marketing*, *professional conferences*, and *strategic relationship-building* to reach target districts. Monthly newsletters, case studies, and annual webinars position CivicRoots as a thought leader in civics education.

2.5 Sales process

Our structured sales process involves initial discovery conversations, customized proposal presentations, and a clear follow-up and contracting timeline of three to six months. We aim for five new district partnerships annually, and strive for a 90% retention rate.

2.6 Pricing strategy

Pricing is strategically based on our delivery costs, market benchmarks, and perceived customer value. We maintain transparency and flexibility in pricing, offering volume discounts and phased implementations to accommodate districts with budget constraints.

2.7 Scaling and operations

We have established clear operational roles, including a Director of Partnerships and dedicated Program Managers for each district partnership. Standardized onboarding and

CRM tools ensure effective project tracking and scalability as we expand regionally and nationally.

2.8 Mixed funding model

CivicRoots leverages *earned revenue* for core operational stability, and uses *philanthropic funds* for new initiatives, curriculum development, innovation pilots, and subsidizing access for under-resourced schools.

Our financial model will transition from 70% philanthropy / 30% earned revenue to an even balance (50% each) within three to five years.

Conclusion

CivicRoots is positioned to significantly expand its impact through a balanced, strategic financial model. By thoughtfully integrating earned revenue with philanthropy, we ensure sustainability and broaden access to quality civics education, fostering a more equitable and engaged democracy.

ACKNOWLEDGMENTS

WHILE THIS BOOK carries my name on the cover, it would not exist without the wisdom, generosity, and brilliance of so many others. I'm profoundly grateful to everyone who helped bring *Mission Meets Market* to life.

To my family—thank you. Your patience, love, and encouragement carried me through the long nights and early mornings that went into this project. I'm especially grateful to my wife, Seema, and my sons, Ryan and Dylan, for reminding me why this work matters.

To my partners at EdSolutions, Jeff Livingston and Beth Mejia—thank you for your vision, belief, and unwavering commitment to helping nonprofits succeed on their own terms. From the earliest conversations to the final edits, your fingerprints are on every page. Your leadership helped build the foundation for this book, and your trust made it possible to write.

To the entire EdSolutions team—this book is yours as much as it is mine. You've helped shape the ideas, test the tools, and refine the methods that make up the MissionMarket Model. You've brought this work to life in partnership with hundreds of nonprofit leaders across the country.

Special thanks to Jaya Yoo, who leads our nonprofit practice and has played an essential role in developing and shaping this model. Jaya's insights, conviction, and deep partnership with clients have elevated every dimension of this work.

To Trish Landeg, Jessica Gersh Wylie, Nicole Parma, and Lily Grabill—thank you for delivering this work every day with care, clarity, and heart. You embody what it means to support nonprofits with excellence and integrity.

To Margo Wright and Andrea Scheive—thank you for the countless hours you've spent translating this framework into tools and learning experiences that empower leaders across cohorts and contexts. Your ability to synthesize, structure, and scale our thinking has expanded what's possible.

To Alex Vinci, To-Nasia Cohen, and Aidan Davis—thank you for building the operational processes that make this work replicable and reliable. Your behind-the-scenes efforts ensure our nonprofit clients are supported as they grow and scale.

To Allison McNamara, Ilse Wolfe, and Sue Tauer—thank you for grounding this work in insights from the field. Your research, through interviews, surveys, and thoughtful inquiry, ensures we stay rooted in the lived experiences of our clients.

To Mackenzie Flynn, Natasha Mir, Jonathan Perry, Erin O'Leary, and Paul Neenos—thank you for working so closely with foundations to ensure our efforts drive real, scalable impact. Your thoughtfulness and strategic guidance have been essential to making this work matter at the system level.

To Emily McLane, who leads our research team, and to her teammates—Anjeli Doty, Bailey Duhé, Samantha Larkin, Janaye McGrew, Tracy Neiman, Tochukwu (Tochi) Okoye, Casey Stisser, and Shirley Zhang—thank you for the rigor and curiosity you bring to every project. Special thanks to Tracy Neiman, who authored the companion workbook, and to Casey Stisser, who supported editing and fact-checking for the book.

To former colleagues Nikkie Zanevsky and Lea Ferguson—your leadership was instrumental in defining and building our approach to Market-Informed Impact®. You helped lay the groundwork for this book's core framework, and I'm grateful for your enduring influence.

To Scott MacMillan, Andrew Tracy, and the editorial team at Grammar Factory Publishing—thank you for helping this book find its voice. Your feedback, structure, and care made the writing clearer and the message stronger.

And finally, to the funders and nonprofit leaders we've worked with—thank you for inviting us into your world. You've challenged us, trusted us, and helped us learn. You've shown us what's possible when mission and market meet with integrity.

ABOUT
THE AUTHOR

JAY BAKHRU is a founding partner at EdSolutions, an education-focused consulting firm that helps nonprofits grow, scale, and sustain their impact.

With more than twenty years of experience across classrooms, startups, and large organizations, Jay brings a practical, well-rounded perspective to the challenges nonprofit leaders face. He started his career as a middle school teacher, later co-founded and led a nonprofit education venture, and served as head of K–12 marketing at a national education publisher.

Jay holds degrees from Brown University (BA), the Wharton School at the University of Pennsylvania (MBA), and Teachers College at Columbia University (MA in Education Policy), where he wrote his thesis on how market dynamics shape K–12 innovation and entrepreneurship.

What motivates Jay is a simple question: How can we get better solutions into the hands of the people who need them most? He believes market forces—used thoughtfully—can help advance equity at scale. *Mission Meets Market* is his way of sharing lessons learned, offering real-world tools to help nonprofit leaders navigate complexity with confidence.

Jay lives in Princeton, New Jersey with his wife and two sons.

ABOUT
EDSOLUTIONS

EDSOLUTIONS IS a mission-driven consulting firm that helps education nonprofits grow their impact and build lasting sustainability. We work across the education continuum, partnering with foundations, nonprofit leaders, and public agencies to design and scale solutions that improve outcomes for historically underserved students.

Our approach is grounded in two proprietary frameworks: Market-Informed Impact®, and the MissionMarket Model. These are strategy tools developed through years of fieldwork to help nonprofits align mission and market, navigate growth, and make strong financial decisions.

To date, we've supported hundreds of organizations— ranging from school networks, to curriculum providers, to advocacy groups—serving millions of students across the country. Our team includes former teachers, nonprofit leaders, policy experts, researchers, and strategists, all united by a commitment to equity and excellence.

If this book resonates with your work, we'd love to hear what you're building. Learn more at www.edsolutions.com.